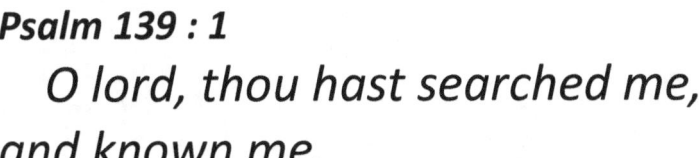

:)

Psalm 139 : 1
O lord, thou hast searched me, and known me.

'God has <u>not</u> forgotten You'
The Workbook
available online at www.PhyllisL-Miata.com

God Has Not Forgotten You

Copyright ©2011, 2017, 2020 by Phyllis Austin, L-Miata

Phyllis L-Miata
2107 N. Decatur Rd. Suite 110
Decatur, GA 30033

All rights reserved. This book, or parts thereof, may not be reproduced in any form without written permission from the author.

Library of Congress Catalog Control Number: 2011905689

ISBN 978-0-9759917-3-2

Printed in the United States of America

Neither the author nor publisher assume any responsibility for the use or misuse of information and sources contained in this book.

Scriptures from KJV unless otherwise stated.

Contact Author:

Email: QueenMiata@onenationenlightened.net
I answer all my emails personally and try to respond within a timely fashion.

Additional books can be ordered online at
www.PhyllisL-Miata.com

Contributing to the
Phyllis L-Miata
Legacy

Dedications:

To Demetrius Austin, my best partner in parenting.

To my children for their spirits, and if it wasn't for them, this book probably would have never been written at least not by me. Once you read the introduction you will know why.

Lastly, a special dedication to the people whose purpose is to uplift and resurrect the Spirit of God in our youth.

Acknowledgements:

First and foremost, I give GOD the glory for his grace, love, and vision.

I thank a host of parents and students in the manifestation of this vision.

Since the original publication of this book,
I have learned the following about Our Stolen Legacy
pertaining to terms used in this book:

Upon the conquering of KEMET by the Greeks in 332 BC:

1) KEMET (KMT) was changed to Egypt (Greek word).

2) GOD (Greek word) meaning power replaced NTR/Neter (Kemetic word) meaning the Divine Force within. **https://youtu.be/RmKRZJxOmEg**

~ *Queen Phyllis L-Miata*

CONTENTS

Foreword: Choosing this book   9
Introduction: Life lessons not chapters   13

LIFE LESSONS

One: You are *'of GOD'*   15

Two: *You are the only one who can place limits and boundaries on you*   39

Three: *You have the Power of Choice*   67

Four: *Honour Thy Mother and Father*   79

Five: *Ignorant Behavior is not Adult Behavior*   87

Six: *Forgive, Trust, and Be Patient*   103

Seven: *God has not forgotten YOU*   129

DAILY AFFIRMATIONS FOR THE STUDENT   144

Other Products by Phyllis L-Miata   147

Foreword
Choosing This Book

Thanks for choosing this book. Though I will not believe to know why you selected this particular book, *SPIRIT* has told me many will choose this book because there is a void existing within self, an unfulfilled emptiness.

Here's something you need to know. When I first sat down to write this book, I already decided on its title, *'You Can Control Your Destiny'*. However, near completion of the book, God gave me his title, *'God Has Not Forgotten You'*. It was towards the end of writing this book when I truly understood why. At that point, I wrote this foreword.

Spirit wants me to tell you, "Stop looking for something to fill the void." Many only think of the negative emotions associated with a void, i.e. the feelings of being unloved, lonely, unwanted, etc. Nonetheless, there is a positive reward given upon the existence of a void. When a void dwells inside one, one is presented with *'the opportunity to create'*. In other words, you don't have to look for something with which to fill the void, *You Can Create It*."

> Genesis 1:2
> *And the earth was without form, and void; and darkness*

> *was upon the face of the deep. And the Spirit of God moved upon the face of the waters*

When there existed a void in the world, God created the heavens and the earth. And, He created You.

God has not forgotten you. He knew you before you were born. Your life is precious regardless of the appearances of turmoil, abandonment, trials, tribulation, etc. You are here for a reason, a purpose.

> *Psalm 139; 13-16 (New Living Translation)*
> *You made all the delicate, inner parts of my body and knit me together in my mother's womb.*
> *Thank you for making me so wonderfully complex! Your workmanship is marvelous—how well I know it.*
> *You watched me as I was being formed in utter seclusion, as I was woven together in the dark of the womb.*
> *You saw me before I was born. Every day of my life was recorded in your book. Every moment was laid out before a single day had passed.*

God has not forgotten you. Thus, any void that exists in you comes with a blessing, a great reward. It allows for your 'ability to create' to be put to work.

> *Genesis 1:27*
> *So God created man in his own image, in the image of God created he him; male and female created he them.*

> *Genesis 1:28*
> *And God blessed them...*

Therefore, in times of discomfort, know that you were made in the image and likeness of God. Know that God has blessed you. Know that you have the Power to create, and know that God, our God, your God, has not forgotten you.

Introduction
Life Lessons not Chapters

I decided to write this book as a manual for my children. I wanted to leave them something emphasizing the life lessons I hope they will learn. It was during my children's teenage and young adult years, I found myself repeating, re-emphasizing and re-addressing lessons over and over again. Asking, *"Don't they get it? Why would they want to learn it the hard way, through personal suffering, the school of hard knocks?"* At that moment, I said, *"I am going to just write a book, hand it to them, and tell them to refer to the lesson(s)."*

    I knew the idea of writing a book was not just a fleeting thought. What I did not know was the intensity of the commitment. The replay of teenagers' and young people's stories in my mind was an endless movie. I connected with what I wanted my children to learn and remembered what many teenagers and young adults were not taught or forgot. Adults and parents were not excluded. As I heard and saw the actions of adults and parents, I apprehended the reality of not knowing basic truths and their effects resonating in hopelessness, despair, victimization, etc.

    As the journey of writing this book took its course, I knew the goal was to convey to the reader the understanding that the school of hard knocks and experience along are for fools. My goal is to develop a wiser person who knows one can predict where he/she will be tomorrow based on the present mind-set. As such, there are vital spiritual life lessons one must follow for self to live, heal, renew and reach its purpose.

There are seven chapters, i.e. seven life lessons in this book. The spiritual meaning of the number seven is completion. According to *Christian Resources Today,* the number seven has also been used when describing the covenant between man and God.

When I sat down to write this book, I had no idea of the structure (life lessons) or the length (7 chapters) of the book.

However, Spirit did.

Life Lesson #1
You are 'of GOD'

You are "of GOD"

In our first lesson, we will look at how you identify yourself - your identity. This is very important because you act out your identity everyday. Your identity is a subconscious ruler and dictator of your actions.

Let us begin.

Again, your first life lesson is: You are ***'of GOD'***. GOD created you.

As God created the Universe, He imagined and brought into physical manifestation a vision that reflects His image – YOU.

> Genesis 1:26
> And God said, Let us make man in our image, after our likeness: and let them have dominion...over all the earth...

> Genesis 1:27
> So God created man in his own image, in the image of GOD created he him; male and female create he them.

> Genesis 2:7
> And the Lord GOD formed man of the dust of the ground,

and breathed into his nostrils the breath of life; and man became a living soul.

Yes, YOU are made in the image and likeness of GOD. That's right, purely stated, you are *'of GOD'*, yes YOU.

Accordingly, our first life lesson is that your identity is *'of GOD'*. When you identify yourself as *'of GOD'*, you have identified your unlimited power. Inherently, there are no boundaries on you. You can accomplish everything.

Now, I want you to look in the mirror. Ask yourself, *who are you? How do you identify yourself? Are you identifying yourself based on what you see, your physical characteristics? Are you identifying yourself based on how others in society see you, or are you identifying yourself based on a higher power?*

Real Story 1
When I meet with women, mostly parents, who soon will be released from the local county jail, I ask them to write down how they identify themselves. Other than a few comments such as recovering addict, recovering alcoholic, etc., many of the characteristics are similar to parents in my other support groups. In the following list, are some given characteristics:

I am a God-fearing person...
I have faith...
I am a person who is steadfast...
I have made mistakes, but I am trying hard to correct them...
Overall, I am a good person, hard working...
 etc.

To the parents who use more negative personifications, I say to them, "Identifications like recovering addict, thief, recovering alcoholic, etc. are terms of what you do." To the parents who have more positive images of their identities, I tell them, "You are limiting GOD."
    I constantly remind parents and youths of the 'Truth' - what

they do is not who they are.

One can identify one's self based on:

How one looks?
What one does?
Where one is born?
Who birth one?
How one feels?
Who created one?
etc.

Thus, the obvious inquiry becomes: *How are you identifying yourself?*

(Think)

Which of the above questions gives one the identification associated with the greatest Power in the universe?

(Think)

I recall when a group of teenagers said to me, "Mrs. Austin, they say we are bad." I told the group of teenagers, "You are not bad, you may do bad things. However, you are '*of GOD*'. Therefore, you have the choice to do good things."
      Again, *You have the choice to do good things.* (Choice – the Power to decide…We will discuss 'choice' later in the book.)

Now, it is time for your first exercise.

Exercise 1
Write your identities according to these questions: *How you look; What you do; Where were you born; Who birth you; and Who created you.*

Here are some possible answers:

How one looks: I am tall, dark, Black, White, short, light, male, female...
What one does: I am a doctor, lawyer, gay, straight, recovering addict, husband, wife...
Where one is born: I am an/a American, European, African, Chinese, etc...
Who birth me: I am the son of Mr. and Mrs. Smith, I am adopted, I am the last child of Ms. Jones, etc...
Who created me: I am a child *'of GOD'*. **(*'Of GOD'*)**

You must understand what took place when you were conceived. Before multi-allele genes determined your skin color, before dominant-recessive traits created your eye color, before DNA from your mother and DNA from your father combined and interacted with one another to determine your height, intelligence, unique traits, and characteristics, etc., and before the possibilities of mutations occurred, the sperm fertilized the egg and you were conceived.

Yes, **YOU** were conceived, not the color of your hair, not the sexual identity you will claim, not your ethnicity, not your eyesight or hearing ability, just YOU. The spirit of GOD, the creator, brought your spirit into human awareness and the process began to encapsulate that Spirit within a human being.

Real Story 2
My daughter asked me, "Mom can't we be Black and of GOD' at the same time?"

My answer to her was a resounding 'NO'. I continued..."One minute we are Nigger, Colored, Negro, Black and African American. You are not how others describe you with their limited vision based on outer characteristics; you are of who created you, the GOD who used HIS <u>unlimited power</u> to create you. **You are 'Of GOD'.** "

There are times when I need to reshape this statement to others who do not recognize that the body is just a covering. I tell them: you are not just Black, you are not just a doctor; you are not just a girl, teenager, student, husband, mother, or father. You are *'of GOD'*.

You must understand that the body is just a shell for the Spirit of YOU, which is connected to and part of the Spirit of GOD.

Laugh Out Loud (LOL) moment 1
Because we are so used to hearing terms describing us as characteristics and of what we do as our identity, it may be difficult to grasp this concept. What do you think about the following identifications? I am *'widow's peak'*, I am *'go to the bathroom daily'*, I am *'finger burn'*, etc.

> *Remember....*
> *Genesis 1:27*
>   *... God created man in his own image, in the image of GOD created he him; male and female create he them.*

As was then, and is now, and will be forevermore, YOU are **'of GOD'**.

Let's continue.

There are two parts of YOU...*the Body and the Spirit*

Fig. 1-1 ©2004 Woman and Man, created by God, connected to one another and to Spirit

> *Genesis 2:7*
>   *And the Lord GOD formed man of the dust of the ground, and breathed into his nostrils the breath of life; and man became a living soul.*

'Soul' is often defined as the Spiritual part of humans, distinctly separated from the physical body.

In the literal sense, there are two parts of you: the body and the **Spirit of GOD**.

When GOD blew into man the breath of Life, he gave man his Spirit. And...it is the **Spirit of GOD** within man that gives man his life.
     The Body is just a shell, a casing, which houses God's Spirit. Spirit is the '**of GOD'** part of man. The Body is the physical form, but <u>**it is the SPIRIT that formed the Body.**</u>

Therefore, I ask you...

Which one is greater, more powerful, more creative and more in tune with GOD?

Which one do you want to lead you, the body or the Spirit?

Which one, the body or the Spirit, will give you life?

    James 2:26
       For as the body without the spirit is dead...

Regardless of how your body was formed, it was formed for the purpose of God's Spirit to be demonstrated through you.

The **'of GOD'** part of you connects you to the Source, GOD— the God of *ALL* resources: *Faith, Love, Strength, Wisdom, Power, Imagination, Understanding, Will, Order, Zeal, Renunciation,* and *Life* (According to Charles Fillmore, these are known as the Twelve Powers of Man – twelve expressions of divine power inherent in each of us). It is this part of YOU, *the Spirit of GOD within you,* which gives you your unlimited unconstrained unrestricted ability.

Real Story 3
A teenaged girl told me about her relationship with her mother, father,

and step-father. She mentioned how her mother and stepfather were divorced. She pointed out how her step-father treated her differently from the other children.

What the girl revealed to me next caused her to break down and cry. She said, "My cousin on my father's side would see me and ask why I wasn't at the family gathering? I would reply that I didn't know about it. You know, Ms. Austin, (stating as she started to cry) my mother is the only person I have. I wouldn't know what to do if I lose my mother. I used to go over my father's house when my grandmother was alive; he would be there. He wouldn't say anything to me…as if I didn't exist. He wouldn't even acknowledge me."

I listened to this Child of GOD, which was what she wanted, and I realized, she needed.

To the readers who can empathize with this young lady, I want you to know that…*before you were born, GOD ACKNOWLEDGED YOU as <u>HIS</u> CHILD, and you inherited resources and abilities.* These were the gifts that your **Father GOD** gave to YOU as his heir.

> Romans 8:16
> The Spirit itself beareth witness with our spirit, that we are the children of God:

> Romans 8:17
> And if children, then heirs; heirs of God, and joint-heirs with Christ; if so be that we suffer with him, that we may be also glorified together.

Note: suffer (synonyms: experience and go through)

YOU are a child *'of GOD'*.

Your God father knew to give you *GOOD GIFTS*, gifts that would take you through any trial or tribulation. Your GOD father knew to give you *GOOD GIFTS* that you could seek and find at any time to overcome obstacles and live a life in which all your needs and desires are met and fulfilled. Your GOD father gave you the *GOOD GIFTS* of: Faith, Love,

Strength, Wisdom, Power, Imagination, Understanding, Will, Order, Zeal, Renunciation, and *Life*.

You are *'of GOD'*. You have been acknowledged. Your existence on earth is not a mistake. God's Spirit runs through you. You have the Gifts, you just have to open them and use them.

Always remember: You have a father. You have a father name **GOD**; the **GOD** of all fathers and **HE** <u>acknowledges</u> YOU. God has not forgotten you.

Continuing...

Real Story 4
I was sitting in a restaurant when a former student recognized me. She introduced me to her son and stated, "I told him he has to do good in school because he already has two strikes against him...he's black and he's a boy. Right?"

As she waited for my response, I thought about how to phrase and express my answer for her level of comprehension. I replied, "You know, I never told my son that. I always told him he was a child of GOD and not to limit himself based on how others classify him."

> YOU must always remember:
> ## You are *'Of GOD'*.

Gifts necessary to overcome fear and frustrations...
Because of your true identity being *'of GOD'*, you have been given gifts to use.

One of my favorite scriptures is **2 Timothy 1:7**, which states: **For God hath not given us the Spirit of Fear, but of Power and of Love and of a Sound Mind.** In this scripture, we find the gifts necessary to overcome fear and frustration; fear and frustration are paralyzing thoughts, which limit people. God has given you Power, Love and a Sound Mind to overcome the controlling thoughts of fear and frustration.

In this mind-set, let us take a closer look at these gifts. Throughout the book, we will discuss these gifts in greater detail, giving greater meaning and appreciation.

The Gift of *POWER*

> Genesis 1:26
>
> *And God said, Let us make man in our image, after our likeness: and let them have dominion over the fish of the sea, and over the fowl of the air, and over the cattle, and over all the earth, and over every creeping thing that creepeth upon the earth.*

And, he gave you *Dominion (synonyms: Power and Authority)*

Power is energy, which Creates: One uses Power to bring thoughts into visions and visions into visible manifestation.

At this time, at this present moment, you must appreciate the Power you have to create. YOU must know, understand and grasp the concept that there are only two categories of things you can create. You have the power to create life and those things contributing to and enhancing life. You also have the power to create death and those things that contribute to and enhance death.

Why? Because the origin of what we create can start in the body or in the *Spirit of GOD*, which is within. Those things created and originating in and from the body, will be limiting life-ceasing thoughts and actions. In contrast, those things created and originating in and from the *Spirit of GOD* within, will be un-limiting life-enhancing thoughts and actions.

The easiest way to use your Power to create is by what you choose to think and say.

> *Proverbs 18:21*
>
> *Death and Life are in the power of the tongue: and they that love it shall eat the fruit thereof.*

Power is used to create. YOU have the POWER to Create.

Here's a reality: You have the power to create whatever you are thinking about at this moment.

Exercise 2
Write down your thoughts as they relate to the POWER of creation. Ask yourself: *Do you want to create the present thoughts in your mind?* In addition, focus on what you have said in the last 24 hours and if they fall under creating/enhancing life or creating/enhancing death.

As you will learn in Chapter 2, you 'act-out' your thoughts. In essence, you will create what you are thinking, sooner or later – subsequently shaping your environment. If you don't want to create those thoughts, you must change or eliminate those thoughts.

The Gift of <u>LOVE</u>
> Ephesians 2:4
>> But God, who is rich in mercy, for his great love wherewith he loved us,

Love is energy, which Shapes: One uses love to shape an object or being.

There are five types of love:

        1. Epithumia Love – Physical Desire

        2. Eros Love – Romance

        3. Storge Love – Natural Affection

        4. Phileo Love – Cherished Friendship

        5. Agape Love – Unconditional Love

Agape Love

Epithumia, Eros, Storge, and Phileo loves require the sense or feeling of affection, passion. However, Agape love is unconditional. It is Agape love that operates by choosing to love, choosing to be loving towards others.

Many people will seek love and seek to love based on their feelings. Conversely, there are fewer people who know the true power of Agape love, loving another individual unreservedly and without expectations. Agape love requires a greater spiritual realization because Agape love represents the love God has for us.

Agape love is a choice, not a feeling, and God has chosen to love us – unconditionally.

> *2 Thessalonians 2:16*
> *Now our Lord Jesus Christ himself, and God, even our Father, which hath loved us, and hath given us everlasting consolation and good hope through grace*

Once YOU treasure GOD's unconditional love for you and its shaping of you, you will value the Power you have to shape others through unconditional Love.

> *1 John 4:16*
> *And we have known and believed the love that God hath to us. God is love; and he that dwelleth in love dwelleth in God, and God in him.*

One can choose to love all the time, regardless of feelings, motivations or other emotions. When one practices this type of love, one is demonstrating Agape love. Agape love is the type of love one must practice with others. There may be moments when you may feel like you do not or can not love another. Nevertheless, love means devoutness. You must always have the commitment to exhibit love and the loyalty to act lovingly towards others.

As a being **'of GOD'**, you have been entrusted to love as GOD loves

you.
> *1 John 4:7*
> *Beloved, let us love one another: for love is of God; and every one that loveth is born of God, and knoweth God.*

Love is used to shape. YOU have the *'Power of LOVE'* to Shape. Use your *Power of Love* to shape a life.

Exercise 3a
Write and discuss how it feels when someone unconditionally loves you? How do you feel knowing/remembering that GOD unconditionally loves you? How are you shaped? How can you shape or how do you believe one is shaped when one is unconditionally loved?

Understanding the types of Love

Agape' Love
As stated earlier, Agape love is the type of Love God has for you. Agape' love is a devotional love. Agape' love is a committed love. Agape love is a love of loyalty and a love without conditions.
If you have ever questioned whether or not you are loved, you are. God's love is unconditional, and God devotedly and fervently is committed to loving you. God is loyal in his commitment in loving you.

Agape' love is the type of love parents are to have for their children. God has entrusted a Spirit in his blessings to the parents, **YOU**.

Agape' love is the type of love that parents <u>must</u> exhibit with their children.

Agape' love is the type of love that <u>must</u> exist between husbands and wives.

Agape' love is the type of love we <u>must</u> practice with one another.

One's recognition and acceptance of GOD stipulates the elicitation of God's loving action from the GOD spirit of YOU within you.

Of the five types of Love, Agape' love is the only one rooted in devotion, commitment, loyalty, and fidelity. Why? Because Agape' love is a Gift from GOD. Agape' love comes from the GOD's spirit within You. When you pledge to love in Agape' love, GOD's love is radiating from that part of YOU connected to God's Spirit.

Epithumia, Eros, Storge, and Phileo loves
Epithumia, Eros, Storge and Phileo loves develop out of emotions. Webster defines emotion as *'the affective aspect of consciousness, a state of feeling, a conscious mental reaction (as anger or fear) subjectively experienced as strong feeling usually directed toward a specific object and typically accompanied by physiological and behavioral changes in the body'*. Therefore, Epithumia, Eros, Storge and Phileo loves do not originate in the Spirit of God that is within you but in the body. These emotional loves, which are initiated in the body, are temporary without devotion or commitment. These loves emotionally come and can emotionally go.

I often come in contact with young people who are very casual and loose in their sexual relations. Many do not see a problem in having sex. Some will defend this practice as *'all teens have sex'*. Although I know this not to be true, the willingness of teens to justify their behavior based on the risk others have taken is self-destructive, to say the least. When I respond with a simple truth, which sooner or later one will face, these students' dispositions noticeably sink into a state of abyss. I say, *"One day you will count the number of sexual relations you have had with people who do not want to commit to you, people who could probably care less whether you live, die, catch a disease, etc. How does that make you feel?"*

It is very important for one to understand the difference between love that is derived from God's Spirit and love that has begun in the body.

Many times teenagers are disappointed when they realize that the emotional type of love given them does not have longevity, devotion, commitment, fidelity or loyalty. Fairly speaking, many adults are taken aback when a passionate, heart throbbing, tinkling, toe curling, stomach queasy, love making love is not automatically accompanied by a committed Agape' love.

More upsetting is when the act of premarital sex is not a pledge of commitment, an unborn child to unwed parents is not a declaration of devotion on behalf of the parents and the practice of shacking or custom of marriage is detached from the vow of fidelity.

Exercise 3b
Write about an Eros, Epithumia, Storge or Phileo love towards you that you assumed was accompanied by an Agape' love and how you felt. How do you feel knowing that you are not to assume one is pledging Agape' love?

The Gifts to create a SOUND MIND: <u>KNOWLEDGE, UNDERSTANDING, and WISDOM</u>
> Exodus 35:31
> And he hath filled him with the spirit of God, in wisdom, in understanding, and in knowledge, and in all manner of workmanship

A SOUND MIND is energy, which Illuminates. One must choose to operate with a Sound Mind and not in confusion or chaos. One uses a SOUND MIND to illumine and enlighten.

A SOUND MIND is obtained through the acquisition of knowledge, understanding, and wisdom. When one is using a SOUND MIND, one is transferring knowledge, understanding, and wisdom to the person and/or the situation. Knowledge, understanding, and wisdom are the gifts one has inherited to function in a sound mind.

Knowledge - knowledge is information.

Understanding – understanding is to comprehend the meaning of knowledge.

Wisdom – wisdom is the ability to use knowledge in good judgment/decision making, having insight, astuteness, and intelligence. More importantly, when one uses wisdom, one is radiating life.

> Proverbs 2:6
> For the LORD giveth wisdom: out of his mouth cometh

knowledge and understanding.

Ecclesiastes 7:12
For wisdom is a defence, and money is a defence: but the excellency of knowledge is, that wisdom, giveth life to them that have it.

Proverbs 4:7
Wisdom is the principal thing; therefore get wisdom: and with all they getting get understanding.

It matters not the amount of knowledge one has; what matters is one's understanding of the knowledge and the ability to employ it in a wise intelligent manner with good judgment.

I never will forget what a wise older lady said to me:

People operate at their highest level of Understanding.

In my field, which has allowed me to work around many especially teenagers, when I notice chaotic and foolish behavior, a few minutes of dialogue reveals the mimicking of the person's level of understanding.

There is a profound statement in the movie the *Matrix*: 'One is incapable of choosing beyond their level of Understanding'.

(Think)

Once more, **A SOUND MIND** illuminates. When YOU have knowledge, understanding, and wisdom, YOU are transformed; YOU can operate in SOUND MIND and not in chaos or confusion. YOU have the Power to enlighten others and enhance their life.

Exercise 4
List issues or thoughts about which you are confused and/or without a clear understanding. Now, I want you to list information you need to acquire. How do you feel after writing down the knowledge/

information you need.

Knowing what knowledge is needed is a start. However, you must be about the business of going and getting the knowledge. Next, find out the meaning of the knowledge and how to use it. Don't forget to input wisdom. These are the steps in getting to A SOUND MIND to make decisions.

As you educate your mind with knowledge, understanding and wisdom, you create A SOUND MIND to make sound decisions.

A SOUND MIND edifies, creating sound decisions and uplifting others by putting those sound decisions and their knowledge, understanding, and wisdom into the world; remember, sound decisions are based on knowledge, understanding, and wisdom.

A SOUND MIND is energy, which illumines. You have the POWER to illumine and enlighten others.

Exercise 5
At this time, write about what and how you can illumine the world and/or someone.

Overall
To overcome fear and frustration, one must develop a resolution using a Sound Mind. The resolution/strategy is developed out of knowledge, understanding of the knowledge, and wisdom. In addition, you must be well rested; your energy level must be high to create and implement a resolution. Attack the problem with love not anger. One cannot afford to spend energy being angry; you must reserve that energy to develop a strategy.

> *2 Timothy 1:7*
> *For God hath not given us the Spirit of Fear, but of Power and of Love and of a Sound mind.*

Gifts necessary to move mountains...
God has given you gifts to move mountains, challenges from your life.

The Gift of _FAITH_
> Matthew 17:20
> And Jesus said unto them, Because of your unbelief: for verily I say unto you, If ye have faith as a grain of mustard seed, ye shall say unto this mountain, Remove hence to yonder place; and it shall remove; and nothing shall be impossible unto you.

Faith is energy, which believes, visualizes and imagines: One uses faith to stay hopeful in one's belief. Hope can ground a person in Faith.

How do we use the scripture of Matthew 17:20?

First: Unbelief is not recognizing that there is a *Spirit of GOD*. Therefore, you must believe and be aware of the *Spirit of GOD* within you. For faith is given to us by GOD not man. Thus, the man who doesn't believe there is a *Spirit of GOD* will be faith deprived. And, the man that operates from the body (flesh) is a natural man, he too will be faith impaired.

> 1 Corinthians 2:14
> But the natural man receiveth not the things of the Spirit of God: for they are foolishness unto him: neither can he know them, because they are spiritually discerned.

It is the *Spirit of GOD* within *you* to which you must turn to remove the mountains and challenges from your life; you are limited in trying to resolve/remove the challenges (mountains) based on your physical ability (your body, your flesh).

> John 6:63
> It is the spirit that quickeneth; the flesh profiteth nothing: the words that I speak unto you, they are spirit, and they are life.

> James 2:26
> For as the body without the spirit is dead, so faith without

works is dead also.

Secondly: Faith is a vision, an image, which one can imagine and has the belief of it coming into visible manifestation.

> *Hebrews 11:1*
> *Now faith is the substance of things hoped for, the evidence of things not seen.*

Faith and *Imagination* are spiritual gifts given to you by GOD. Imagination is very important. The gift of imagination allows you to visualize an ending and create a vision. The vision of an ending is what you must continue to see, believe and hope for with the mind's eye as you work towards your vision. YES, YOU MUST WORK YOUR FAITH.

Your vision can be modified and restructured as you work your faith, varying with your work level. Simply put, the relationship between work, vision and faith is: *The Greater the Vision, the Greater the Work; the Greater the Work, the Greater the Faith.*

> *James 2:20*
> *But wilt thou know, O vain man, that faith without works is dead?*

> *James 2:17*
> *Even so faith, if it hath not works, is dead, being alone.*

In other words: The vision that you have will not come into visible manifestation (become real) without hard work. Without hard work, your vision is *'dead'*.

Let's continue.

Strength is one of God's gifts to us. The definition of Strength is a source of power and energy (the ability to do work). The Spirit of GOD within possesses strength.

2 Samuel 22:33
God is my strength and power: and he maketh my way perfect.

Exodus 15:2
The LORD is my strength and song, and he is become my salvation: he is my God, and I will prepare him a habitation; my father's God, and I will exalt him

Ephesians 3:16
That he would grant you, according to the riches of his glory, to be strengthened with might by his Spirit in the inner man;

One taps into strength by merely asking GOD in prayer and believing. HIS strength gives you the energy and power to begin and continue the work.

Judges 16:28
And Samson called unto the LORD, and said, O Lord God, remember me, I pray thee, and strengthen me, I pray thee, only this once, O God, that I may be at once avenged of the Philistines for my two eyes.

1 Samuel 28:22
Now therefore, I pray thee, hearken thou also unto the voice of thine handmaid, and let me set a morsel of bread before thee; and eat, that thou mayest have strength, when thou goest on thy way.

Luke 22:32
But I have prayed for thee, that thy faith fail not: and when thou art converted, strengthen thy brethren

Lastly: The more work one performs in working towards the vision, the more POWER one has to create. As you work through faith in GOD, the *Spirit of GOD* within you comes forth in a mighty way.

> Matthew 21:21
> Jesus answered and said unto them, Verily I say unto you, If ye have faith, and doubt not, ye shall not only do this which is done to the fig tree, but also if ye shall say unto this mountain, Be thou removed, and be thou cast into the sea; it shall be done.

Your GOD Identity, your Father GOD's Gifts to you...
GOD created you. You are '*of GOD*'. And, it is *the Spirit of GOD* within you, which gives you your unlimited unconstrained unrestricted ability.

> Acts 6:8
> And Stephen, full of faith and power, did great wonders and miracles among the people.

> Revelation 2:26
> And he that overcometh, and keepeth my works unto the end, to him will I give power over the nations:

The gifts are interlocking. At times, one gift may seem separate from another, but it is not. All gifts and their usage start with Love, Unconditional Love – **AGAPE' LOVE**.

1 Corinthians 13 (Amplied Bible)

> ¹IF I [can] speak in the tongues of men and [even] of angels, but have not love (that reasoning, intentional, spiritual devotion such as is inspired by God's love for and in us), I am only a noisy gong or a clanging cymbal.
>
> ²And if I have prophetic powers (the gift of interpreting the divine will and purpose), and understand all the secret truths and mysteries and possess all knowledge, and if I have [sufficient] faith so that I can remove mountains, but have not love (God's love in me) I am nothing (a useless nobody).

³Even if I dole out all that I have [to the poor in providing] food, and if I surrender my body to be burned or in order that I may glory, but have not love (God's love in me), I gain nothing.

⁴Love endures long and is patient and kind; love never is envious nor boils over with jealousy, is not boastful or vainglorious, does not display itself haughtily.

⁵It is not conceited (arrogant and inflated with pride); it is not rude (unmannerly) and does not act unbecomingly. Love (God's love in us) does not insist on its own rights or its own way, for it is not self-seeking; it is not touchy or fretful or resentful; it takes no account of the evil done to it [it pays no attention to a suffered wrong].

⁶It does not rejoice at injustice and unrighteousness, but rejoices when right and truth prevail.

⁷Love bears up under anything and everything that comes, is ever ready to believe the best of every person, its hopes are fadeless under all circumstances, and it endures everything [without weakening].

⁸Love never fails [never fades out or becomes obsolete or comes to an end]. As for prophecy (the gift of interpreting the divine will and purpose), it will be fulfilled and pass away; as for tongues, they will be destroyed and cease; as for knowledge, it will pass away [it will lose its value and be superseded by truth].

⁹For our knowledge is fragmentary (incomplete and imperfect), and our prophecy (our teaching) is fragmentary (incomplete and imperfect).

¹⁰But when the complete and perfect (total) comes, the incomplete and imperfect will vanish away (become antiquated, void, and superseded).

¹¹When I was a child, I talked like a child, I thought like a child, I reasoned like a child; now that I have become a man, I am done with childish ways and have put them aside.

¹²For now we are looking in a mirror that gives only a dim (blurred) reflection [of reality as in a riddle or enigma], but then [when perfection comes] we shall see in reality and face to face! Now I know in part (imperfectly), but then I shall know and understand fully and clearly, even in the same manner as I have been fully and clearly known and understood [by God].

¹³And so faith, hope, love abide [faith--conviction and belief respecting man's relation to God and divine things; hope--joyful and confident expectation of eternal salvation; love--true affection for God and man, growing out of God's love for and in us], these three; but the greatest of these is love.

You are *'of GOD'*
Live Your GOD identity every God given moment.

Life Lesson #2

You are the only one who can place limits and boundaries on you

You are the only one who can place limits and boundaries on you.

In our second life lesson, we will discuss how one can place boundaries and limits on one's self.

As stated earlier, it is my belief and experience that people live their identity each and every day. What one does, speaks, tries, accomplishes, etc., is based on how one identifies one's self. Therefore, a person's day to day thoughts can be limiting or non-limiting.

> *Proverbs 23:7*
> *For as he thinketh in his heart, so is he: Eat and drink, saith he to thee; but his heart is not with thee.*

In layman's term:

Thoughts become Words, Words become Actions, Actions create Habits, and Habits build Character, Character shapes YOUR LIFE.

I have written this book because of my day to day experiences with teenagers who already have been defeated in life, and they don't know it. I have listened to teenagers for years; I have taught them over the years. And, I have concluded that there exists a never ending downward spiral of self-identity in a countless number of teenagers. Too many teenagers' self-identity has disintegrated to what only is seen in the mirror and what others think. Some personas are enthralled in sexual desires. Yet, others focus their uniqueness being the clothes their wear. Such identifications are limiting; such identifications create boundaries and such identifications produce low expectations.

As a person, you feed your subconscious mind with thoughts. If you feed your subconscious mind with limiting thoughts (going in), limiting results will manifest (come out).

One of my objectives to you, the reader, is to help you realize the importance of understanding your true specialness – a being of God. It is this distinctiveness that allows you to play a vital role in controlling your destiny. Hence, you must know the limits and boundaries you place on yourself start with how you identify yourself.

> *Proverbs 23:7*
> *For as he thinketh in his heart, so is he...*

Accordingly, you are the only one who can place limits and boundaries on you.

Real Story 5
There were times, as a substitute teacher, when I would be placed in a chaotic class. During such times, I would often ask students to write down their identity, how they identify themselves. I remember doing this activity when one young man shouted, "I am a nigger. We are all niggers up in here." Then he stated, "I am using the term in the positive sense, Nigga not Nigger."

Subsequently, I asked the most obvious question. "What is positive about the word Nigga?" I added, "You can write your comments as they relate to the present time or history." I followed with, "What enlightenment and resources do you have access to based on that identification?" I continued. "What is your standard of practice, the way you carry yourself and the way you conduct your business based on that identification?" Lastly, my inquiry was, "What are you

YOU ARE THE ONLY ONE WHO CAN PLACE LIMITS AND BOUNDARIES ON YOU

entitled to or is there any inheritance due you based on that identification.

Exercise 6
Based on your identification of you, I want you to answer the following questions:
1) *What is positive about the words and terms you selected?* If necessary, you may want to define the words/terms.
2) *What part of you is enlightened and illuminated by your identification?*
3) *What resources do you have access to and are connected to your identification?*
4) *What are your standard of practice, the way you carry yourself, and the way you conduct your business based on your identification?*
5) *What are you entitled to or is there any inheritance due you based on your identification?*

One side note: In real story number #5, the young man's paper remained blank.

As we continued the class, a hearty debate developed on how the young man's standards and expectations of others, especially his fellow classmates, were based on the color of their skin.

I remember growing up knowing and having instilled in me, *'I can do anything I set my mind to because I was created by GOD.'* My parents connected my identity to *'the SOURCE'*, **GOD.** Not only did I have access to all their belongings and teachings, but I was given acquisition to the best resources they couldn't give me, GOD's resources. And, because of God's resources, I could do anything.

Because I have God's resources, I grew up knowing...

> *Philippians 4:13*
> *I can do all things through Christ which strengtheneth me.*

My mother often conveyed her wisdom to me - as with the time she taught me always to use my God-given common sense and not to fear any man, especially one who could not walk on water.

Several years ago, I found the scripture echoing those words.

> *2 Timothy 1:7*
> *For God hath not given us the Spirit of Fear, but of POWER, and of LOVE, and of a Sound Mind.*

Reader, the '*of GOD*' identity within YOU has connected you to the source of all resources, allowing you to move past limiting thoughts and actions.

Before any recognizable characteristics based on your earthly parents' DNA developed in you while in the womb of your mother, GOD gave you HIS spirit of Power, Love, and Wisdom to overcome all fear and frustration, and GOD gave you Faith and Imagination to move and remove any mountainous objects. Best of all, the gifts that GOD gave you allow you non-limiting non-restricting non-constraining abilities.

HIS *Power*, HIS *Love*, HIS *Wisdom* are already within you, inborn and inherent GOD-given spiritual faculties including *Faith, Strength, Imagination, Understanding, Will, Order, Zeal, Renunciation,* and *LIFE.* When you allow the Spirit of GOD to work through you, there is nothing you can't do. And, in spirit, there is nothing too hard for GOD.

> *Jeremiah 32:17*
> *Ah Lord GOD! Behold, thou hast made the heaven and the earth by thy great power and stretched out arm, and there is nothing too hard for thee.*

Let's examine our connection to the resources based on our identification...
If my parents are rich and could buy anything, guess what? I can buy anything. All I have to do is ask. Still, my parents may institute some guidelines, which I must follow to use their resources. However, if I follow the given guidelines, I have access to the resources when I ask

and in most cases when I don't.

For example, when I was younger and lived in my parents' house, I had access to the resources in the home. Simply by having the identity of being my parents' child, I had access to their resources: house, transportation, health care, support, love, etc.

Most of the things I wanted, I had access to: piano lessons, drama lessons, skates, etc. Also, there were those things I would get if I would follow certain guidelines: use of the car, money beyond allowance, trips, etc. Regardless of what it was, if they had it, I had access to it because my identity connected me to their resources.

In my adult life, I realized that some things I needed weren't always had by my parents. But, because of their wisdom of *'Whose'* they are, children of GOD, they knew how to get it. Therefore, they taught me that I am a child *'of GOD'*. My mother's exact words were, *"You may have come through me, but YOU are 'of GOD' "*. Because of this, all of GOD's resources, whatever you want or need, are available to you. You are not limited.

It was around 13 years of age when I learned that I was given certain gifts just because I was *'of GOD'*. Those gifts, I was told, were the 12 POWERS OF MAN outlined in chapter one: *Faith, Love, Strength, Wisdom, Power, Imagination, Understanding, Will, Order, Zeal, Renunciation,* and *Life*. From the age of 13, my mother, for the rest of her life, in some shape, form or fashion, reminded me of the gifts and gave guidance on using them.

Whenever I would face a challenge, a wall or a limit, I turned within to Spirit. In my life, I can honestly say that a challenge, a wall, and a limit never became a boundary or limitations.

Guidelines
Remember when I said sometimes my parents may institute guidelines?

Here were the guidelines:

1. Think before you speak. You can't say everything you think. Watch what you think and what you say.
2. Use your God-given common sense.

3. Fear no-one who can't walk on water.

As I grew, I learned the Spiritual translations:

1. You have the Power to Create with your thoughts and words.

    Proverbs 18:21
    Death and Life are in the power of the tongue: and they that love it shall eat the fruit thereof.

2. Implement Wisdom and seek knowledge and understanding.

    Proverbs 2:6
    For the LORD giveth wisdom: out of his mouth cometh knowledge and understanding.

    Ecclesiastes 7:12
    For wisdom is a defence, and money is a defence: but the excellency of knowledge is, that wisdom, giveth life to them that have it.

    Proverbs 4:7
    Wisdom is the principal thing; therefore get wisdom: and with all they getting get understanding.

3. Don't give in to Fear.

    2 Timothy 1; 7
    For God hath not given us the Spirit of Fear, but of POWER, and of LOVE, and of a SOUND MIND.

In addition, I realized that as a teenager:

- -I was being taught and groomed to move in the world with un-limitless...
- -I have the POWER, the energy, to create my Destiny...
- -I have the POWER to create and remove limits and boundaries...

YOU ARE THE ONLY ONE WHO CAN PLACE LIMITS AND BOUNDARIES ON YOU

POWER in God's Creations
GOD gave everything he made his Spirit, and in doing so he gave everything he made His POWER.

> *Genesis 1:1*
> *In the beginning GOD created the heaven and the earth.*

And the Earth and its waters were created...
> *Genesis 1:2*
> *And the earth was without form, and void...And the <u>SPIRIT</u> of GOD moved upon the face of the waters.*

We can find the <u>SPIRIT</u> of GOD in the Powerful Earth

Figure 2-1. The Earth

To the Earth...a marvelous creation...
The energy associated with the Earth is called geothermal. The word geothermal comes from the Greek words geo (earth) and therme (heat). Accordingly, geothermal energy is heat from within the earth. Steam and hot water produced inside the earth can be used for heat or generate electricity. Geothermal energy is a renewable energy source; the water is replenished by rainfall and the heat is continuously produced inside the earth. Geothermal energy is generated in the earth's core, about 4,000 miles below the surface. Temperatures hotter than the sun's surface are continuously produced inside the earth. Temperatures may reach over 9,000 degrees Fahrenheit.

The Earth's crust is broken into huge plates (refer to figure 2-2.) that move apart or push together at about the rate of a few centimeters per year. Convection of semi-molten rock in the upper mantle helps drive plate tectonics.

What the scientific community now calls the Asian Tsu-

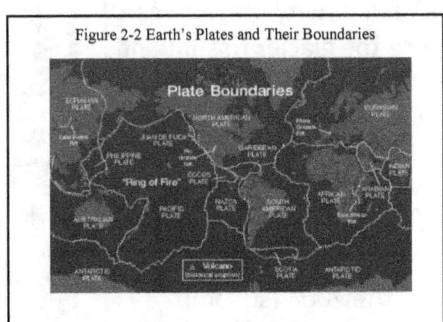
Figure 2-2 Earth's Plates and Their Boundaries

nami (Japanese word that means "harbor wave.") occurred as a result of an earthquake in the Indian Ocean on December 26, 2004. The epicenter was off the west coast of Sumatra, Indonesia. The earthquake was cause by a tectonic shift. One statistic emerging from the data is that the power of the tectonic shift was equivalent to over 8,000 nuclear bombs.

We can find the <u>SPIRIT</u> of GOD in the Powerful Waters:

Fig. 2-3. Water and its movement against rocks

To the children of Egypt, step into the waters, and the waters will part...
The waters of the Earth cover seventy-five percent of the Earth's surface. The term hydro refers to water. Hydropower and Hydroelectric power are produced from water. The use of water to produce power started thousands of years ago, i.e. using water to turn water wheels for grinding wheat into flour. Water turbines are use to generate electricity. As we move further into the Green revolution, there is a push to create more hydropower vehicles.

    The force of water rushing over riverbanks is minor. On a larger scale, the force of Earth's water continues to reshape Earth's crustal plate. For example, the Grand Canyon was carved by water. The frozen force of water can build and form ice called glaciers. The glacier grows bigger and heavier as more snow and ice attach to it. The weight of the glacier and the force of gravity on Earth can cause the glacier to shift and move. Everything in the path of a glacier (trees, rocks, and even mountains) can be moved. In Figure 2-4, you will note the reshaping of Banda Aceh by water after the 2004 tsunami.

Fig. 2-4. The before and after pictures of Banda Aceh, which was reshaped by the 2004 Asian Tsunami.

YOU ARE THE ONLY ONE WHO CAN PLACE LIMITS AND BOUNDARIES ON YOU

And the Sun, the Moon, and the Stars were created...
> Genesis 1:3
> And GOD said, LET there be light: and there was light.

> Genesis 1: 16-18
> And GOD made two great lights; the greater light to rule the day, and the lesser light to rule the night: he made the stars also.
> And GOD set them in the firmament of the heaven to give light upon the earth.
> And to rule over the day and over the night, and to divide the light from the darkness: and GOD saw that it was good.

We can find the <u>SPIRIT</u> of GOD in the Powerful Sun:

Fig. 2-5 The Sun beaming over the Earth.

To the Sun, which has risen above the Earth...
The Sun is a star. It is the closest star to Earth. The Sun is the largest object in our Solar system, containing 99.8 percent of the total mass in the Solar System. The strong gravitational pull of the Sun holds Earth and the other planets in the solar system in orbit.

The temperature on the Sun's Surface is 5,800 Kelvin. At the core of the sun, the temperature is 15.6 million Kelvin and the pressure is 250 billion atmospheres. At the center of the core the Sun's density is more than 150 times that of water.

The Sun's energy output is about 4 billion billion megawatts. Our largest power plants produce around 5,000 Megawatts of power. Each second about 700,000,000 tons of hydrogen are converted to about 695,000,000 tons of helium and 5,000,000 tons of energy in the form of gamma rays. Another way to look at this is that the sun puts out every *second* the same amount of energy as 2.5×10^9 of those large power plants would put out every *year*---wow, over two billion! As it travels out towards the Earth's surface, the energy is continuously absorbed and re-emitted at lower and lower temperatures so that by the time it reaches the Earth's surface, it is primarily visible light. For the last 20% of the way to the Earth's surface, the energy is carried more by convection than by radiation.

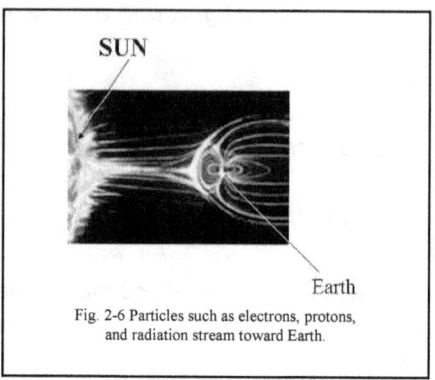

Fig. 2-6 Particles such as electrons, protons, and radiation stream toward Earth.

The Sun is the source of heat, which sustains life on Earth, and controls our climate and weather. Weather patterns and rainfall are determined by the reaction between the sun's energy and the Earth's atmosphere. The tilting of the Earth towards the sun creates the seasons. The Sun's energy is associated with photosynthesis, which helps plants to grow, and the Sun's role in biodegradation helps complete the natural cycle of ecosystems. Solar energy use by plants is the root of most of the other forms of energy humans use for power. In addition, wind power depends on the sun's impact on atmospheric movement to create wind patterns. In essence, the sun allows life to exist.

We can find the <u>SPIRIT</u> of GOD in the Powerful Moon:

Fig. 2-7 The Moon

To the Moon, which light the night...
On to us, the Moon reflects the Sun's light. The Moon orbits around the Earth and is our only natural satellite. The Moon's average distance from Earth is 384,400 km and its temperature range is from -171C to 111C. There is a gravitational pull on the moon approximately one-sixth that of Earth because the moon is much smaller than the Earth.

You probably know gravity pulls all objects towards the Earth. Hence, the moon stays in orbit because of Earth's gravitational pull on the moon. Conversely, the moon exhibits a gravitational pull on the earth, which affects the moving waters. The power of the moon's gravitational force affects the waters, and the waters are pulled towards the moon - tides are created. What else? Tidal Energy is electricity produced from harnessing energy from tides.

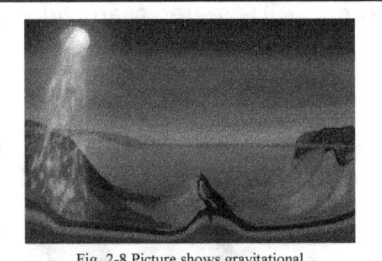
Fig. 2-8 Picture shows gravitational pull on Earth

We can find the SPIRIT of GOD in the Powerful Stars:

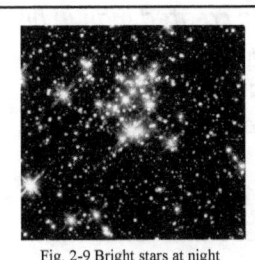
Fig. 2-9 Bright stars at night

To the night that reveals thousands of little stars...
Stars are born within the clouds of dust and scattered throughout most galaxies. Stars are large balls of gases that emit their own radiation. As the cloud collapses, a dense, hot core forms and begins gathering dust and gas. Not all of this material ends up as part of a star — the remaining dust can become planets, asteroids, or comets or may remain as dust. A star the size of our Sun requires about 50 million years to mature from the beginning of the collapse to adulthood. Our Sun will stay in this mature phase for approximately 10 billion years.

Stars are fueled by the nuclear fusion of hydrogen to form helium deep in their interiors. The outflow of energy from the central regions of the star provides the pressure necessary to keep the star from collapsing under its own weight, and the energy by which it shines. Moreover, stars are responsible for the manufacture and distribution of heavy elements such as carbon, nitrogen, and oxygen, and their characteristics are intimately tied to the characteristics of the planetary systems that may coalesce about them.

NOTICE :
ALL God's creations being made of <u>SPIRIT</u> and <u>POWER</u>, as are YOU. You have been created with Spirit and Power. YOU have been created to be Spiritual and Powerful.

Then, GOD created Man and Woman...

Fig. 2-10 Woman and Man, created by God, connected to one another and to Spirit.

And GOD created man to posses POWER and ENERGY.

As God created the Universe, He imagined and brought into physical manifestation a vision that reflects His image...YOU.

Genesis 1: 27
So God created man in his own image, in the image of God created he him; male and female created he them.

Genesis 1: 28
And God blessed them, and God said unto them, Be fruitful, and multiply, and replenish the earth, and subdue it: and have 'dominion' over the fish of the sea, and over the fowl of the air, and over every living thing that moveth upon the earth.

And, God gave you *Dominion,* which means *Power and Authority:*

GOD gave POWER to everything. Everything GOD made has the POWER and energy to create. Everyday, GOD's creations use their GOD given POWER to create.

What about man?

What about YOU?

What does man do?

What do YOU do?

YOU ARE THE ONLY ONE WHO CAN PLACE LIMITS AND BOUNDARIES ON YOU

THINK!

One day, as I sat meditating, a spiritual meaning entered my heart with full understanding. In John 5:11, Jesus says, *"Arise, Take up thy bed, and walk"*. This verse resonated in my heart as a metaphor for one having a role in creating one's condition and the power to create one's destiny.

In this day of wastefulness, the following is a saying I make to young men.

> GOD gave man two hands to help him create Greatness and all he does is hold up his pants?
> -Phyllis Austin

Do you wake every morning understanding you have the Power to create and implement resolutions, move and remove mountains, create and enhance life, and determine your Destiny?

(THINK)

> *Remember-*
> *Your beliefs become your thoughts. Your thoughts become your words. Your words become your actions. Your actions become your habits. Your habits become your values. Your values become your destiny.*
> -Mahatma Gandhi

Limiting Thoughts

ALL of GOD'S creations, including man, including YOU, have POWER. GOD didn't make anything weak or inferior. GOD's creations are of order. GOD didn't make anything out of chaos or confusion, including you. YOU are of order.

GOD gave you the gifts. Those gifts were inborn inherited gifts from GOD. One must realize that everything opposite the Gifts (12 powers of man) are limiting thoughts leading to limitations and boundaries. Refer to the table 2-1.

Table 2-1

Limiting Thoughts	Opposite	God's Gifts: Twelve Powers of Man
Doubt/Fear	instead of	FAITH
Hate, Fear	instead of	LOVE
Weakness/Fragility	instead of	STRENGTH
Foolishness/Imprudence Folly	instead of	WISDOM
Inferiority/Fear	instead of	POWER
Sight/ Concreteness	instead of	IMAGINATION
Not seeking knowledge & understanding/State of Ignorance/Fear	instead of	UNDERSTANDING
Indifference Thoughtlessness Lethargy	instead of	WILL
Chaos/Confusion	instead of	ORDER
Stativity/State of Acceptance	instead of	RENUNCIATION
Apathy/Lethargy	instead of	ZEAL
Death/Destruction	instead of	LIFE

Thoughts, words, and actions surrounding doubt, fear, hate, weakness, foolishness, inferiority, sight, ignorance, lethargy, chaos, confusion, stativity, apathy, death and destruction cause limitations and create boundaries. Less realized is that these thoughts were learned. They are not a part of our nature as we were created by GOD.

If you have embedded and conditioned in you these thoughts, you can unlearn them and recondition yourself. One can start by refusing to be ignorant. Seek knowledge and understanding.

Real Story 6
It is not unusual for me to hear teenagers complain about school. I hear statements like: why do I have to learn this; this is stupid; when are we going to use this; people don't act like that; you know black people; that what's wrong with white people; Asians are smart; etc. My favorites are: you can't do that, and I didn't know.

I love to share my knowledge with them. I generally start by saying, "You know, there are an estimated 6 billion people in this world and seven continents." Then I show them a globe. I start naming countries, discussing various cultures and changes in the world that I have witnessed. I continued with, "Have you ever thought that in making those statements, you are saying you know everything about the world, its people, and its future? In addition, the implication is that your future and destiny in relationship to the world and its people are exclusively known by you."

In a roundtable discussion, with colleagues, on how teenagers don't want to be held accountable for what they don't know, but refuse to learn what they don't know a new word was coined – 'stup-ignorant'.

Ponder on the following:
> *"He who knows not and knows not he knows not: he is a fool - shun him. He who knows not and knows he knows not: he is simple - teach him. He who knows and knows not he knows: he is asleep - wake him. He who knows and knows he knows: he is wise - follow him."*
>
> *- Persian Proverb*

Reader, ignorance is the opposite of knowledge. When one engages in refusing knowledge, one is creating and operating in a state of *'Stup-ignorance'*.

More importantly, knowledge is the foundation of understanding and wisdom. Knowledge, understanding and wisdom are the building blocks for creating a SOUND MIND. Your choices in life need to be made with a SOUND MIND.

When you limit your knowledge, you limit your ability to make the best informed choices. Therefore, not only is rejecting knowledge upholding ignorance, but one is engaging in a limiting action contributing to limited choices and limited outcomes.

> *Proverbs 10:14*
> *Wise men lay up knowledge: but the mouth of the foolish is near destruction*

Exercise 7
*Referring to the following list below, which limiting thoughts and actions have you engaged in the past week.
*List: *doubt, fear, hate, weakness, foolishness, inferiority, sight, ignorance, lethargy, chaos, confusion, stativity, apathy, death, destruction...*
*Write the limitation or boundary caused/created.

Physical POWER
As a teenager, taking a physical science course, you may have learned Physical power this way, *Physical Power is energy, and energy is the ability to do work.*

Mathematically: power = *work/time*, work= *Force x distance and* Force= *mass x acceleration*.

Simply speaking, the more energy you have, the more POWER is associated with YOU. However, physical power is limited by physical boundaries. Fundamentally, what you are capable of doing, seeing, hearing, understanding etc., restricts your power.

In essence, your physical power is in-line with the body, and the body is limited.

SPIRITUAL POWER
According to God's greatness and his Spirit gifted in you, you have something more than physical power. GOD has given YOU his POWER; in essence, you have **GOD'S Power…**and, **God's power is** Spiritual power. Spiritual power promotes sight to vision and thoughts to imagination. As you start to recognize your Spiritual Power, you envision unseen images. When you operate in Spiritual Power, you are working your works based on faith that GOD will deliver, one day these images will be created.

How do you tap into GOD's Power?

You tap into GOD's POWER through Faith.

> *1 Peter 1:5*
> *Who are kept by the power of God through faith unto salvation ready to be revealed in the last time*

> *Revelation 2:26*
> *And he that overcometh, and keepeth my works unto the end, to him will I give power over the nations:*

Limiting Experiences
Many teenagers have gone through difficult and sometimes atrocious experiences: molestation, incest, starvation, physical abuse, etc. Some have suffered the loss of parents, family members or become orphans instantaneous. Others are going through illnesses and depression.

One who has been victimized by rape is not a rape victim but was and is still 'a child *of* GOD'. The rapist may have taken the body, but the rapist cannot touch the spirit. That 'of GOD' part of one can only be given away, not taken.

Thus, the way GOD created you is AWESOME. GOD created you so that no-man has POWER over <u>all</u> of you. The body is just a shell, a casing of the YOU inside. The *Spirit of GOD* is your identity. The

Spirit of GOD can live on even after natural death. We see this in Rev. Dr. Martin L. King Jr., Mahatma Gandhi, and others.

You must understand that you are a Spiritual Being. Limitations and boundaries are created when you move as a Physical being, a human being, a man, or woman. Your non-limiting, non-restricting, non-constraining power is in Spirit not in man.

> *1 Corinthians 2:5*
> *That your faith should not stand in the wisdom of men, but in the power of God.*

In the movie, *The Last Airbender*, a profound statement was made about the Avatar. One villain said to the other, both of whom wanted the Avatar, *'Don't kill him (the Avatar), he will just reincarnate anyway, and we would have to search for him again...'*

Your non-limiting, non-restricting non-constraining power is in the Soul - the Spiritual part of man. The Soul transcends the natural death; the Soul can never be killed nor can it die.

Suicide (Overcoming suicidal thoughts and tendencies)

Suicide is a limiting thought. Suicidal thoughts and attempts develop when one has failed to see a way out in the natural world. At the time one has suicidal thoughts and tendencies, one is in the wretchedness of only seeing man's way as having or providing an out, a solution.

The American Academy of Child and Adolescent Psychiatry gives the following warning signs of adolescents who may try to kill themselves:

* change in eating and sleeping habits
* withdrawal from friends, family, and regular activities
* violent actions, rebellious behavior, or running away
* drug and alcohol use
* unusual neglect of personal appearance
marked personality change
* persistent boredom, difficulty concentrating, or a decline in the quality of school work

* frequent complaints about physical symptoms, often related to emotions, such as stomachaches, headaches, fatigue, etc.
* loss of interest in pleasurable activities
* not tolerating praise or rewards
* complain of being a bad person or feeling "rotten inside"
* give verbal hints with statements such as "I won't be a problem for you much longer;" "Nothing matters;" "It's no use;" and "I won't see you again."
* put affairs in order, give away favorite possessions, clean room, throw away important belongings, etc.
* become suddenly cheerful after a period of depression
* have signs of psychosis (hallucinations or bizarre thoughts)

Many teenagers want and feel the need for people, parents, and family to express love, care, concern, support, and communication towards them. If you are going through this do <u>all</u> of the following:

* Do not trivialize what you are going through.
* Do not neglect or ignore your behavior.
* Get immediate help, call a hotline.
* Make sure you have a trusting individual in whom to confide, if you don't, turn to **GOD.**
* Be positive and reinforce to yourself that with help *this feeling, I too shall overcome.*

Whether you are a teenager, young adult, parent or child, at the time one is thinking about committing suicide, the thought pattern is that of 'white or black, no gray area.' In others words, one cannot see a way out. It is a tunnel vision of the worst kind. One cannot see over the hill, across the street, or around the corner. The person is thinking that there is no way out, it will not get any better, and it is unbearable.

It is an emotional bondage for everyone when a loved one is in such a state that renders one to kill one's self. When the person is an adult, and even more a parent, guardian, or caretaker, it can be hard to understand why some life lessons - Spiritual life lessons - were not learned, experienced or believed. Life lessons such as:

- ❖ This too shall pass.

- ❖ The Spirit giveth life.

- ❖ If you just hold on, joy will come in the morning.

- ❖ All things work out for those who love the Lord.

- ❖ We shall overcome.

- ❖ Trust in the Lord, with all thy understanding.

- ❖ Cast your burdens upon the Lord.

- ❖ The latter will be better than the past.

- ❖ Galatians 6:8
    For he that soweth to his flesh shall of the flesh reap corruption; but he that soweth to the Spirit shall of the Spirit reap life everlasting

- ❖ The 23rd Psalm
    The Lord is my shepherd; I shall not want.
    He maketh me to lie down in green pastures; he leadeth me besides the still waters
    He restoreth my soul; he leadeth me in the paths of righteousness for his name's sake.
    Yea, though I walk through the valley of the shadow of death, I will fear no evil; for thou art with me;
    Thou preparest a table before me in the presence of mine enemies; thou anointed my head with oil; my cup runneth over.
    Surely goodness and mercy shall follow me all the days of my life; and I will dwell in the house of the Lord for ever.

Many of our parents and grandparents taught us life lessons that helped us to trust in the Lord when we had little faith and could not see tomorrow; it was Black and White. They held on until they saw *Gray*. We must hold on until we see *Gray*. We must help our children, our friends, and others to see *Gray*.

If you need love, remember that you are always loved:
>Romans 8:39
>>Nor height, nor depth, nor any other creature, shall be able to separate us from the love of God, which is in Christ Jesus our Lord.

>1 Corinthians 16:24
>>My love be with you all in Christ Jesus. Amen.

>2 Corinthians 13:14
>>The grace of the Lord Jesus Christ, and the love of God, and the communion of the Holy Ghost, be with you all. Amen

>2 Thessalonians 2:16-17
>>Now our Lord Jesus Christ himself, and God, even our Father, which hath loved us, and hath given us everlasting consolation and good hope through grace,
>>Comfort your hearts, and stablish you in every good word and work.

If it is forgiveness you need, you got it:
>Luke 23: 34
>>Then Jesus said, Father, forgive them for they know not what they do

>Mark 2: 10-11
>>But that ye may know that the Son of man hath power on earth to forgive sins (he saith to the sick of the palsy).
>>I say unto thee, Arise, and take up thy bed and go thy way into thine house.

If you have unbearable sorrow, burdens, or pain, give it to GOD:
>Psalm 55: 22
>>Cast thy burden upon the LORD, and he shall sustain thee: he shall never suffer the righteous to be moved.

1Peter 5: 6-7
Humble yourselves therefore under the mighty hand of GOD, that he may exalt you in due time.
CASTING ALL YOUR CARE UPON HIM, FOR HE CARETH FOR YOU.

Psalms 37: 5
Commit thy way unto the LORD; trust also in him; And he shall bring it to pass.

Matthew 11: 28-30
Come unto me, all ye that labour and are heavy laden, and I will give you rest.
Take my yoke upon you, and learn of me; for I am meek and lowly in heart: and ye shall find rest unto your souls.
For my yoke is easy and my burden is light.

If you need a healing, you got it:
Isaiah 53: 4-5
Surely he hath borne our griefs, and carries our sorrows: yet we did esteem him striken, smitten of GOD, and afflicted.
But he was wounded for our transgressions, he was Bruised for our iniquities: the chastisement of our Peace was upon him; and with his stripes we are healed.

Matthew 8: 16-17
When the even was come, they brought unto him many that were possessed with devils: and he cast the spirits with his word, and healed all that were sick.
That it might be fulfilled which was spoken by E-sá-ias the prophet, saying, Himself took our infirmities, and bare our sicknesses.

YOU ARE THE ONLY ONE WHO CAN PLACE LIMITS AND BOUNDARIES ON YOU

Mark 2: 10-11
But that ye may know that the Son of man hath power on earth to forgive sins (he saith to the sick of the palsy)
I say unto thee, Arise, and take up thy bed and go thy way into thine house.

Matthew 13: 15
FOR THIS PEOPLE'S HEART IS WAXED GROSS, AND THEIR EARS ARE DULL OF HEARING, AND THEIR EYES THEY HAVE CLOSED; LEST AT ANY TIME THEY SHOULD SEE WITH THEIR EYES, AND HEAR WITH THEIR EARS, AND SHOULD UNDERSTAND WITH THEIR HEART, AND SHOULD BE CONVERTED, AND I SHOULD HEAL THEM.

If you feel you will be judged, read:
Luke 6: 37
Judge not, and ye shall not be judge: condemn not, and ye shall not be condemned: forgive, and ye shall be forgiven.

If you have been judged and you have paid the price, it is my belief that once you have changed, once you know that you will not do the things that you've once done, and once you are following the way of the righteous, do not allow others to remind you of the old you.

You did it. You acknowledged it. You paid the price. Now, it is time to move on.

If you need faith, turn to:
Matthew 17: 20
And, Jesus said unto them, Because of your unbelief: for verily I say unto you, If ye have faith as a grain of mustard seed, ye shall say unto this mountain, Remove hence to yonder place; and it shall remove; and nothing shall be impossible unto you.

> Mark 11: 22-26
> And Jesus answering saith unto them, Have faith in GOD.
> For verily I say unto you, That whosoever shall say unto this mountain, Be thou removed and be thou cast into the sea; and shall not doubt in his heart, but shall believe that those things which he saith shall come to pass; he shall have whatsoever he saith.
> Therefore I say unto you, What things soever ye desire, when ye pray, believe that ye receive them, and ye shall have them.
> And when ye stand praying, forgive, if ye ought against any: that your Father also which is in heaven may forgive you your trespasses.
> But if ye do not forgive, neither will your Father which is in heaven forgive your trespasses.

Always remember:
You are not a mistake. Any and all things can be overcome. For GOD truly loves you. We love you. Such is the power of AGAPE LOVE.
Choose now to get the spiritual and human help you need. GOD has a plan for you. Consult *SPIRIT* to find out your plan.

Judgmental actions
Judging others and even self-judgment can be very limiting because one may tend to judge the outcome, the experience, instead of the cause or the consciousness i.e. consciousness → cause → effects/results.

Real Story 7
During my tenure as an administrator in an alternative school, I learned not to be 'quick to judge'. I recall when I told of a story to my family and asked for their comments. I said, "There's a young lady who is a full blown prostitute and has been since the age of 14." I asked my son, "What do you think of that?" My son stated, "She's a HOE." I continued, "Well, her mother and father are both on Crack. And, she didn't want her younger siblings to go to Foster care. Consequently, she started selling her body to provide for her siblings and keep her family

intact. Now, what do you think?"

> Luke 6: 37
> *Judge not, and ye shall not be judge: condemn not, and ye shall not be condemned: forgive, and ye shall be forgiven.*

My experiences have taught me that I am hard on self, sometimes overly embarrassed when I make mistakes and understand the judgment that might come. In addition, I have learned people tend not to judge the cause, just the effect.

When you judge just the effect/outcome, you limit the knowledge and understanding developed through analysis of cause/effect association. In addition, as we have stated before, limited knowledge limits SOUND DECISION MAKING. Judging the effects can also limit the understanding one has about GOD. In essence, instead of judging the experience, one should judge according to the truth about GOD.

Real Story 8:
I have never met a person who believes in GOD, who doesn't believe that GOD is the most powerful force in the world, i.e. omnipotent. However, some of these same people will give more credit to others including but not limited to the enemy/Satan/Devil etc. for their circumstance. Sometimes, I would ask, "But you believe in GOD, right?" Sometimes I would say, "You know, I am not an expert on the Bible, but I believe Jesus cast out devils, and somewhere in the Bible doesn't it say Get behind thee Satan. Now, I could be wrong, but I do remember reading that Satan and the Devil were bound."

According to the Bible:

> *Revelation 19:6*
> *And I heard as it were the voice of a great multitude, and as the voice of many waters, and as the voice of mighty thunderings, saying, Alleluia: for the Lord God omnipotent reigneth.*

Note: Neither does society or you benefit when one fails to recognize and use GOD's power.

Marianne Williamson writes in 'Our Greatest fear' :

> ...Our deepest fear is that we are powerful beyond measure.
>
> ...You are a child of God. Your playing small does not serve the world.
>
> ...We were born to make manifest the glory of God that is within us. ...As we are liberated from our own fear, Our presence automatically liberates others.

Judging an experience according to spiritual understanding is considered to be a righteous judgment.

> John 7:24
> Judge not according to the appearance, but judge righteous judgment.

LOL moment 2
I remember a person who blamed her throat cancer as being tested by GOD. The person was 40 years old and had been smoking since 15 years of age.

Jumping to the Conclusion
There are other times when I have noticed someone *'jump to the conclusion'*. Have you ever posed a question and before you were able to state the question in its entirety, someone gives an answer? Subsequently, the answer has nothing to do with the question, i.e. *limited knowledge in, limited knowledge out*.

> Proverbs 18:13
> He that answereth a matter before he heareth it, it is folly and shame unto him.

Overall
Life is like a journey. Imagine you on a road trip from New York to Los

YOU ARE THE ONLY ONE WHO CAN PLACE LIMITS AND BOUNDARIES ON YOU

Angeles. As you start the journey, you don't know what is ahead: slow traffic, flat tires, bad weather, etc., all representing the trials and tribulations you will go through in life. However, you know you will get there. You only have to see ahead a few feet. One note, you will not arrive at your destination one second sooner than the time you actually get there. You have your plan, and the journey/life has its plan.

Nonetheless, you are the ultimate decider on going forward with the trip. You determine if the flats, road conditions, bad weather, etc. will be enough of a limitation to end the trip. The natural man may have Triple AAA motor club. However, the Spiritual man has GOD – Omnipresent, Omniscience, and Omnipotent.

You are the only one who can place limits and boundaries on you.

Life Lesson #3
You have the Power of Choice

Our third life lesson is: You have the Power of Choice.

Life is full of choices. If you don't make choices in life, life will make choices for you. Therefore, you must remember that *'YOU have the Power of Choice'*.

In this life lesson, one must be able to recognize when given a choice. Unfortunately, one can be so conditioned in being told what to do that one has developed a diminished awareness of given choices. This was the case in the next Real Story.

Real Story 9
Two teenaged students were constantly talking and causing a class distraction. Twice the teacher directed the girls to be quiet. As another alternative, the teacher told one of the students to move to another area in the room. The teacher's exact statement was, "Young lady, you need to move to another location in the room. You can select your seat but you must move - now."

The young lady wanted to argue. She stated, "I'm not talking. I'm not going to move." The teacher firmly replied, "Get up. Move here right now, period." The young lady got up and moved to the pointed chair and sat with her 'mouth poked out'.

The young lady was so trained to being told what to do; she failed to control her destiny when being presented with a choice. The teacher allowed the student to use her 'Power of choice'. Instead, the girl forfeited her 'Power to choose' and gave it to someone else (in this case, the teacher) to choose her destiny.

If you don't make choices in life, life will make choices for you.

Life-Altering Choices
From my experience, some of the most important life-altering decisions are made between ages 13 and 25. Choices made during these years tend to set one's life path and its tone for the quality of life one will have. In addition, many choices are irreversible. Needless to say, great rewards or devastating consequences are manifested at the end of such irrevocable choices.

With limited coping skills and life experiences, many teenagers and young adults make instant mechanical decisions. Others may lack access to the wisdom of an adult, refuse the wisdom of an adult or exhibit an inability to learn from the experiences of others.

Physiologically, all complex tasks such as thinking or forming and responding to emotions, require the involvement of many brain regions. The frontal lobes of the cerebral cortex are where the most complicated forms of reasoning and problem-solving take place. However, the frontal lobe doesn't reach full maturity until around the age of 25. Thus, making cognitive maturity associated with adulthood. Hence, in reality, the teenage and young adult mind is developmentally deprived to engage in rational logical reasoning, which is compounded by the heavy emotional and hormonal changes occurring into the late stage of puberty.

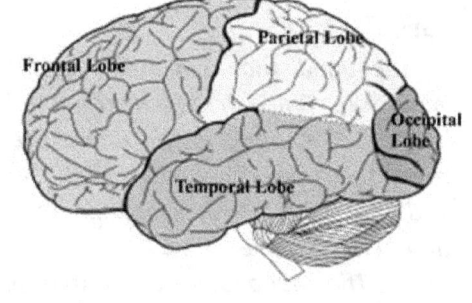

Quite frequently, many parents and caretakers lack this knowledge and adopt a failed parenting strategy of *'hands-off'* or *'let*

them learn from experience'. Parents must realize teenagers are not little adults. Therefore, more appropriate approaches during this age interval involve more explaining, more guidance, more showing and more demonstrations.

For YOU, the teenager or young adult, must access the knowledge and understanding of the wise and learn from other people's experiences. Life is too short to make all the decisions from which you need to learn.

(Reflect on this statement: *I must recognize the experiences of my Mother and Father.*)

I want you to give careful thought to the following real stories. Real stories 10, 11, 12, 13 and 14 reflect on retaliation/revenge decisions.

Real Story 10
A 12th grade female student was very upset when she found out that her boyfriend had another girlfriend in 10th grade. The 10th grade female was pregnant by the boy. A teacher decided to intervene after hearing the story. The teacher told the young lady in 12th grade, "Do not try to compete by having a baby. I have seen this story too many times. Don't do that." Sadly, the teacher's advice came too late. The young lady had informed the teacher that she too was pregnant.

Real Story 11
A young man was constantly being bullied at school. When he told his mother, she stated to him, "You can handle that". The next day, the boy took a knife to school and threatened the student. The boy was eventually expelled from school after a tribunal hearing.

Real Story 12
A young man in the military became very distraught and suicidal after a break-up with his girlfriend, a young lady whom he intended to marry. The destructive behavior caused the military to intervene. The young man's spotless record is now laced with psychological counseling and evaluation.

Real story 13
A male college student was expelled from college and had to serve time in prison. The student was convicted of battery after beating another student who had made a homosexual advance towards him.

Real Story 14
A young lady was being pressured to prove her love to her boyfriend. The young lady engaged in sex with her boyfriend and sent naked pictures via her cell phone. After their break-up, the ex-boyfriend sent the pictures around the school and disclosed the sex acts. The young lady committed suicide. The young man was found guilty of distributing porn.

Real stories 10, 11, 12, 13 and 14 remind us over and over again teenagers'/young adults' tunnel vision aid them in making decisions with severe consequences, which are permanent. To YOU, the reader, your life expectancy in America is approximately 78 yrs. of age. Therefore, see beyond the now. Especially in real story number 12, one must realize that you can't control anyone other than your self and you have a life time to live, love and prosper. Understand that in all challenges you must continue to exhibit love, sanity and respect for self.

Next, real stories 15, 16, and 17 reflect poor decisions in friendship associations.

Real Story 15
Four young men went out for an evening of bowling. Three of the young men had been drinking including the owner of the vehicle who was drunk and sound asleep on the back seat of the car. On the drive home, two of the young men (brothers, the youngest a college student) needed to relieve themselves. The designated driver (a college student) pulled over. The two brothers went in an alley. The younger brother made a comment that it would be funny if they robbed a nearby couple. The older brother disregarded the remark and retuned to the car. The younger brother followed.

Approximately 10 minutes later, the car was pulled over by the police. Guns were drawn. The young men were forced out of the car onto the ground. All were arrested. At the police station, the four were charged with Armed robbery.

After a trial and being found guilty, the two brothers received the maximum amount of time to serve; they had public defenders. The owner of the car served less time; he too had a public defender. The designated driver, fortunately, was able to access good legal representation. He had a cousin who was in Law School. Because of his clean record, the designated driver received probation. His record was expunged after completing probation.

The three young men did not know the younger brother had a gun.

Real Story 16
A 16 year old girl was in love with a young man. The parents of the young girl did not like the relationship and forbade their daughter to associate with the boy. The daughter continued to see the boy without her parents' permission.

The boy picked up the young girl from school. The boy let the girl drive the car. They stopped at a convenience store. The boy went into the store and returned to the car with a soda. The two young people spent the afternoon together at the boy's house, unsupervised, engaging in sex.

Later that evening, the police knocked on the door belonging to the home of the 16 year old girl's parents. The parents were astonished as their daughter was arrested and charged in connection with a crime. The parents, without legal counseling, allowed the daughter to be questioned at the police station. The daughter eventually was convicted and served time in connection with the armed robbery that the boyfriend committed at the convenience store.

The boyfriend never denied his girlfriend's involvement.

Real Story 17
One day, a 14 year age girl walks to the mail box, never to return as the naive youth that she is. For more than seven years, she is exploited as a teen prostitute.

The mother discloses to me that this was not a kidnapping or child abduction. She states, "I later learned that the friends my daughter was associating with from her middle school were recruiting her into prostitution. They convinced my daughter to meet them, and my daughter was gone."

The preceding real stories (15, 16, and 17) are heartbreaking. In my profession, I come across students who question whether one should or can be guilty by association. The question is answered in real story 16 – YES. Many people find themselves in severe circumstances because of their alliances.

One must recognize that the judgment and criterion they use to select friends may be flawed. One must learn and understand the moral value of a person, especially how one identifies one's self. I remember hearing one parent tell his child, *"Don't associate with anyone who has less to lose then you do."* My mother use to tell me, *"You have no friends. Trust GOD."*

Next, real stories 18, 19, and 20 reflect on *Don't Get Even Get Ahead/ Success* decisions.

Real Story 18
A black male student with a 3.7 GPA enters a predominantly white classroom in which he has the highest class average. He sits down, and a group of white students enters the classroom and congregates around him.

A white male student asks, "Do you want to hear a joke?"

Several peers in the group simultaneously reply, "Yes."

The student asks, "What do you call a Black Man wearing a suit?"

(No one responds.)

He then states the answer, "Defendant."

(The students laugh.)

The young man continues, "What do you say to a Black Man wearing a suit?"

(No one responds.)

"Defendant, will you please rise," he replies.

(The crowd laughs.)

The black male student informs the teacher, who does nothing. The next day, the student walks in then out of the classroom. The student goes to inform an administrator.

The administrator recognizes that what had occurred was 'Bullying' and initiated the appropriate consequences for those involved.

Real Story 19
A teenaged foster boy, for a period of approximately two years, engaged in relentless dialogue with a teacher. The teenager's goal was to convince the teacher that he was a good kid and to get the teacher and her husband to adopt him, which they did.

Real Story 20
As a teenager in the 70's and 80's, I always wanted a 1000 watt stereo system. After college, I had the opportunity to buy it. However, computers where changing our society and I had to make a choice. I chose the computer system. It had two 5 inch floppy drives – back then a must. Within a week, I registered and took a Lotus 123 course.

Within one year, after graduating from college, Lotus 123 gave me the competitor's edge I needed to obtain job offers.

> 1 Corinthians 13:11
> When I was a child, I spake as a child, I understood as a child, I thought as a child: but when I became a man, I put away childish things.

I heard of an NBA player who basically adopted the family next door.

The matriarch of the family stated, *"When we went to church, he was right there."*

I remember when I wanted to run away. My mother's wisdom spoke, she stated, *"Think about where you are going."* I customarily tell teenagers, *"I ran away to college."*

Again, YOU have the Power of Choice.

YOU must never give up your power of choice or control of self. In all situations and challenges, you must maintain love, sanity, and respect of self.

Exercise 8
You are making choices all the time. **a)** List 5 choices you have made recently and their consequences (negative or positive). **b)** Try to list at least 3 choices in which you followed your will and ignored your Spirit. If you later learned that Spirit's way was the better way, discuss/write what you've learned.

> *Psalm 33:20*
> *Our soul waiteth for the LORD: he is our help and our shield.*

The Greatness Choice
Choose greatness. Choose GOD.

The Greatest choice one can make is to let the God spirit inside be one's guide. The choice to follow Spirit and not the body is the greatest choice one can make.

> *John 6:63*
> *It is the spirit that quickeneth; the flesh profiteth nothing: the words that I speak unto you, they are spirit, and they are life.*

Remember, your body is a vessel, a casing, a house for God's Spirit. We are all Spiritual beings. As you move through life, the Spirit of God within wants to work magnificently through you.

Will you allow it?

Will you let God's spirit lead and fulfill your life?

If you are following your emotions, your flesh or your body, will you move and change to following your Spirit?

> 2 Corinthians 5:6-8
> Therefore we are always confident, knowing that, whilst we are at home in the body, we are absent from the Lord:
> For we walk by faith, not by sight:
> We are confident, I say, and willing rather to be absent from the body, and to be present with the Lord.

You are the Great decider. You determine whether you will follow the Spirit within. I often set the scenario of walking or driving with a friend. However, the friend is really God's Spirit. As you come across choices, challenges, and obstacles, ask your friend (God's Spirit) for HIS opinion. Seek God's advice. Learn to listen to his advice.

You may have to learn how God's spirit speaks to you. Learn to recognize God's inner voice speaking to you. It may be difficult at first, but if you meditate and quiet yourself, over time you will learn how your GOD's spirit within you speaks to you.

Trust GOD
Earlier I stated that my mother told me, ""*You have no friends. Trust GOD.*" I later learned in life my mother gave me an age appropriate understanding. She planted the seed of solution to challenges, decisions and obstacles. The solution is always within in you. Learn to trust GOD and turn within.

> Proverbs 3:5
> Trust in the LORD with all thine heart; and lean not unto thine own understanding.

We have been created not based on our own understanding, but according to GOD. Therefore, the ultimate plan for our life lies in the creator, GOD. Our understanding lies in the Spirit of GOD within us. In order to get the full understanding that leads and enhances life, we must turn from sight to faith and trust GOD.

> *2 Corinthians 5:7*
> *For we walk by faith, not by sight*

As stated previously, your power lies in GOD. We are here so GOD can work through us and manifest his power. You must allow GOD to be GOD in your life.

> *Proverbs 3:6*
> *In all thy ways acknowledge him, and he shall direct thy paths.*

Here is a thought provoking discussion. What if the first commandment, which is *Exodus 20:3- Thou shalt have no other gods before me,* references the understanding to follow Spirit and not the worldly body? In other words, what if *'no other God before me'* includes the body? Therefore, when and if you choose to follow the body, you put the body before the Spirit of God, which is within you.

Remember the body is just a shell, a covering and a temple, which houses God's spirit within you. Choose for your house (body) to serve the Spirit and be led by the Spirit.

> *Joshua 24:15*
> *And if it seem evil unto you to serve the LORD, choose you this day whom ye will serve; whether the gods which your fathers served that were on the other side of the flood, or the gods of the Amorites, in whose land ye dwell: but as for me and my house, we will serve the LORD.*

Use your Power of Choice.

Life Lesson #4
Honour Thy Mother and Father

Note: Both the biblical and traditional ways of spelling honour/honor are used.

Our fourth life lesson is Honour Thy Mother and Father.
>	*Deuteronomy 5:16*
>>		*Honour thy father and thy mother, as the LORD thy God hath commanded thee; that thy days may be prolonged, and that it may go well with thee, in the land which the LORD thy God giveth thee.*

Subsequently, you are to honour thy mother and father.

Again, our fourth life lesson is *'Honour thy mother and father'*.

In life lesson four, we will discuss what is meant by *'Honor Thy Mother and Father'*. This life lesson tends to educe a variety of comments because of the misinterpretation of the word *'Honor'*. Therefore, let's discuss the meaning of honor. To honor means to recognize. For that reason, when we honor our parents, we recognize their experiences.

For example, an *Honor's* ceremony is given as a way of recognizing one's accomplishments. Similarly, when we honor our mother and father, we recognize their experiences and their accomplishments.

Your parents are examples of which roads to take in life and those to avoid. In recognizing what your parents have gone through, you should not want to repeat the bad, an action elongating your life i.e. *'your days may be long'*.

> *Exodus 20:12*
> *Honour thy father and thy mother: that thy days may be long upon the land which the Lord thy God giveth thee.*

Without a doubt, when we learn from our parents' experiences, we are given the understanding of what is effective and ineffective, what works and does not work, what is useful and is not useful, etc. This information and knowledge, when given to us, aid us in making wise decisions and not being wasteful of time, money, talent and life.

Let's refer back to Real Story 16. In the story, the parents forbade the young lady to see the boy. The young girl disobeyed the parents and severe consequences resulted.

This story is fairly typical. On the surface, one can look solely at whether the child obeyed or disobeyed the parents. However, a more in depth analysis ask the question, *'Did the teenager honor her parents' knowledge, understanding, and wisdom'?*

The short answer is 'no'.

Although we are not privy to the entire dialogue, young people need to realize that their parents and older people have gone through life experiences procuring them the knowledge, understanding, and wisdom of perceptiveness. The adults' discriminatory ability comes with life experiences useful in determining positive and negative tendencies.

In Real Case 16, the parents' insightfulness recognized the boy as a negative entity and influence on their daughter. As teenagers and young people, you need to revere such life lessons, which already have been learned. And, as parents, we need to share these life lessons.

The young lady in Real Story 16 did disobey her parents, but more importantly, she fails to honor them. The young lady fails to identify her parents' life experiences; the effect of that failure leads to incarceration for the young lady. Remember, the young lady was convicted of being involved in an Armed Robbery and sentenced to jail.

Life experiences are reality checks and proofs of probable outcomes subsequent to choices and decisions. Therefore, parents' life experiences give youth knowledge, understanding and wisdom to see beyond sight and perceive highly probable conclusions and aftermaths.

Always remember, the knowledge, understanding and wisdom one gains from honoring one's parents are priceless.

Obey?
Quite regularly teenagers ask, "*Does honor mean to obey?*" Simply put, honor does not mean obey or to obey. If this is so, you may be asking yourself, how did this scripture: *Honour thy mother and father...* come to mean obey thy parents? It doesn't. The scripture that encompasses the word obey and implies its meaning is as follows:

> Ephesians 6:1
> *Children, obey your parents in the Lord: for this is right.*

I want you to repeat the above scripture three times.

Children, obey your parents in the Lord: for this is right.
Children, obey your parents in the Lord: for this is right.
Children, obey your parents in the Lord: for this is right.

Did you recognize that you are to obey parents who are 'in the LORD'?

What does that mean? Think about it.

Earlier, we discussed the body and the Spirit. In the previous chapter (Chapter 3), you were asked to make a choice. The choice was to choose to operate in the body or in the Spirit. When you operate in the Spirit, you are operating in the Lord, i.e. *right in the Lord*.

Thus, if your parents are operating in the Lord and allowing Spirit to guide them, then a child should obey their parent(s).

Next question:

What is meant by Honour and Obey?

Fundamentally, we are to *Honour* our parents - always. We are to *obey* our parents when they themselves are right in the LORD.

Here's an example.

Let's say you have a parent on CRACK cocaine. Honor that parent. Recognize what that parent has done, be it right or wrong, to put him/her in that situation and condition.. In appreciating the parent's life experiences, you are in a position to use the parents' knowledge, understanding and wisdom to make better choices and decisions.

In this circumstance, do you have to obey the parent?

No. Not necessarily.

It is obvious that the parent is being guided by the body's yearning for crack. And, unfortunately, the parent being on CRACK is not *'in the LORD'*. Therefore, the parent's body temple is not receptive to the understanding and wisdom of allowing GOD to lead one.

Now, let's suppose this crack addictive parent tells the child not to use drug. What should the child do? The child should honor the parent by accepting that the parent has certain life experiences, which warrant examination. Based on that assessment, it makes sense not to use drugs.

Regrettably, there are parents who are not parenting and who are not supporting their families. Teenagers and young people may feel angry, discouraged, upset, unwanted, unloved, etc. Because of these hurt feelings, one may wander off the 'Beacon Path' of their purpose in life - DON'T. Don't do something stupid or take the wrong path because of hurt feelings. Remember, the knowledge, understanding, and wisdom you will gain from honouring your parents are priceless. Therefore, set aside these feelings and use the parents' life as substantive information and understanding for making better and wiser choices.

The long term objective of developing a wise man or woman must outweigh the short-term disappointment in a parent. *'Acting in wisdom is to life as acting in foolishness is to death'.*

> *Proverbs 13:14*
> *The law of the wise is a fountain of life, to depart from the snares of death.*

Continuing...

> *Ephesians 6:1-3*
> *Children, obey your parents in the Lord: for this is right.*
> *Honour thy father and mother; which is the first commandment with promise;*
> *That it may be well with thee, and thou mayest live long on the earth.*

When one reads Ephesians 6:1-3, one gets a better contrast between the words Honor and Obey. In these scriptures, to Honour thy father and mother is stated as the first commandment with promise. The promise is *'if you do this, your days will be long'*. Honouring thy mother and father makes sense because you are using and demonstrating knowledge, understanding, and wisdom, which has been acquired. There is no need to make stupid decisions leading to deadly consequences.

Let's continue. Please read.

> *Leviticus 20:9*
> *For every one that curseth his father or his mother shall be surely put to death: he hath cursed his father or his mother; his blood shall be upon him.*

> *Matthew 15:4*
> *For God commanded, saying, Honour thy father and mother: and, He that curseth father or mother, let him die the death.*

Mark 10:19
Thou knowest the commandments, Do not commit adultery, Do not kill, Do not steal, Do not bear false witness, Defraud not, Honour thy father and mother.

Here we learn that the opposite of honour is *'curse'*. When one does not honour one's parents, one curseth one's parents. To honour entails one's approval; to curseth entails one's disapproval. However, the honor and the curse are of the knowledge, understanding, and wisdom.

Hence, when one honours thy parents, one approves of the knowledge, understanding, and wisdom. This endorsement of the knowledge, understanding, and wisdom supports one in choices and decisions, which leads one to their days being long, i.e. long life will manifest.

When one curseth thy parents, one disapproves of their knowledge, understanding, and wisdom. When one disapproves of something, one's tendency is not to use it. Therefore, a child who curseth thy parents disapproves of the knowledge, understanding and wisdom, and as such, will reject and not use the knowledge, understanding and wisdom. As a result, the child's choices and decisions are not supported by learned outcomes of previous life lessons delineated from the parents' knowledge, understanding and wisdom. As such, not only is the child doomed to be wasteful, but the child's choices and decisions can manifest negativity and may result in deadly consequences.

The heart of these meanings is in the results that eventually will follow. When one uses knowledge, understanding, and wisdom in life, the outcomes will be life rewarding and positive. Conversely, when one operates from lack of knowledge (ignorance), lack of understanding (stupidity) and lack of wisdom (foolishness), expect one's days to be in peril and cut short. Remember, ignorance, emotions, and stubbornness will not absolve one from the consequences of their actions.

Real Story 21
A teenager was told that lying closes doors. The mom's exact words were...you either open doors or close doors with what you say.

The teenager asked her teacher if she could go to her locker. Instead, the teenager went to the library to hang-out with her friends. When she returned, the teacher informed her that she would be written-up for cutting class. The teenager was sent to the disciplinary office and given a warning for her first offense. However, the parents pulled the young lady out of a pageant focusing on character.

In meeting with the teacher, while the teenager was present, the mother asked the teacher to state what she thinks of her child and to be honest. The teacher aired that she perceives the girl as someone who would lie. The teacher continued and stated that she would not give the girl permission to go to the locker or leave the class even if the girl declared it as an emergency. Additionally, the teacher stated she would probably not write a letter of recommendation for the girl if asked.

One upside to this story was that the teenager had two months left in the teacher's class. Thus, the teenager had time to demonstrate appropriate behavior and character.

Exercise 9
Part A - In real story 21, the girl curses the parents and does not use the knowledge, understanding and wisdom surrounding lying vs. honesty. List the consequences of the child's lying.
Part B - If you have cursed your parents and suffered negative consequences, list the knowledge, understanding and wisdom not used and the resulting consequences.

> *Proverbs 15:20*
> *A wise son maketh a glad father: but a foolish man despiseth his mother.*

Overall, fundamentally and in spirit, children should honour their parents - always. However, to obey your parents comes with a precondition. Children, *obey your parents* requires that your parents are in the LORD obeying GOD.

Honour Thy Mother and Father.

Life Lesson #5
Ignorant Behavior is not Adult Behavior

Because of today's media blitz, young people often mistake ignorant behavior as adult behavior. For example, mocking, saying what you think, giving unsolicited opinions without knowledge, and the degrading treatment of others are all viewed as grown-up perks. These acts do not represent adult behavior but rather pure ignorance.

Therefore, our fifth life lesson is *'ignorant behavior is not adult behavior'*.

God does not want us to be ignorant and never gave us the gift of ignorance.

> 1 Corinthians 12:1
> Now concerning spiritual gifts, brethren, I would not have you ignorant.

You may ask, *'What is adult behavior?'* Overall, adult behavior incorporates knowledge, understanding. and wisdom.

Remember: knowledge, understanding, and wisdom are spiritual gifts; ignorance is not.

> *Exodus 35:31*
> *And he hath filled him with the spirit of God, in wisdom, in understanding, and in knowledge, and in all manner of workmanship*

To my young sisters and brothers, I do not want you to be or act ignorant. And, this is why our fifth life lesson is *'Ignorant Behavior is not 'Adult Behavior'*.

Here are the criteria for *Adult Behavior*.

Adult behavior...
Adult behavior is conscientious of the risk and consequences of actions.
Adult behavior recognizes self-responsibility.
Adult behavior understands the effects on others.
Adult behavior teaches and is empathetic to others.
Adult behavior attempts to do no harm.
Adult behavior understands that today is preparation, a stepping stone, for tomorrow.
Adult behavior should recognize *'home court advantage'*.

Again, spiritually speaking, adult behavior incorporates knowledge, understanding and wisdom and attempts to uplift the person or situation to a higher level of knowledge, understanding and/or wisdom.

Real Story 22
On a family outing to the museum, a teenaged son requested the keys to the car. He claimed that he had been to the museum many times and was bored. His mother denied the request. Upset, her son mocked her and walked away. (She recognized that this was a test.)

> *The mother waited until they arrived home, and told her husband, "I got this." She went into her son's room and verbally drilled into him.*

> > *She told him that mocking and degrading people are easy; I thought I raised you better than that. She continued speaking, "You are too*

unique and too intelligent to resort to such low-grade behavior. What did you prove? Did you prove you could back talk? Wow! That really is amazing. You proved absolutely nothing. You didn't prove that you could negotiate a deal. You didn't prove that you could look beyond the appearance of things and make the best out of a situation you didn't like. You didn't prove that you could be open-minded. You basically demonstrated a lack of maturity and made me realize that I've given you a lot of unearned credit.

    You know, I'm somewhat disappointed. I know you are smarter than what you recently demonstrated. Here you are an 'A' student with nearly 1300 on the SAT (maximum score 1600), and scholarships at hand, and yet you act like that - ignorant. That is not how someone with your credentials and potential acts. That is unacceptable, and that is unintelligent."

    She resumed, "Did you think I would allow you to talk to me like that? What were you thinking? Did you think I would act ignorant when you act ignorant? No. If I had acted like that, you would think that is how people should act, and it is not.

    I will tell you this; you will not talk to me any type of way. I can lovingly make your life hard. First of all, the only thing that requires electricity in this house is the refrigerator. I will disconnect everything. You will have the basics while everybody else will have better.

    You see, I have plenty of time to teach you a lesson, and I will...

She continued with this pattern of reaffirming his uniqueness and telling him the truth about his behavior. After lecturing, the mother and father began teaching their son a lesson he would never forget, a lesson on the difference between appropriate adult behavior and ignorant behavior.

> Proverbs 12:15
> The way of a fool is right in his own eyes: but he that hearkeneth unto counsel is wise.

Reader, the mother waited until they got home. She waited for home court advantage (a secret she learned from her mother). Her son could not go anywhere. He was a captive audience. From that point on, every time her son played a regular card, the parents played a trump card, i.e. when he made an adult move, they met it with an adult responsibility and/or consequence. It took a month to break him (as older people use to say) of his misunderstanding of adult behavior.

> 1 Peter 1:14
> As obedient children, not fashioning yourselves according to the former lusts in your ignorance.

To teenagers and young adults, ignorant behavior is not adult behavior. Littering, cursing out people , fighting, using and taking advantage of people, not taking care of your responsibilities, not taking care of your children, not working while being able to work, and verbally, physically, and emotionally abusing people are <u>all</u> ignorant behaviors. These actions do not contribute to being a responsible adult with integrity and character.

Real Story 23
At a football game, a parent began to tell me the story of her encounters with several staff members at her child's school. The parent told her story and stated, "I had to go off on them to get what I wanted."

She asked me for advice. My first comment was, "I understand the issue is frustrating. In order to get what your child needs, you must start with understanding that going off is not a negotiating skill. "

Later, in the conversation, the parent disclosed that she is still coping with the problem, looking for resolution.

IGNORANT BEHAVIOR IS NOT ADULT BEHAVIOR

Ignorant behavior does not incorporate wisdom and is the behavior of fools...

Ecclesiastes 10:3
Yea also, when he that is a fool walketh by the way, his wisdom faileth him, and he saith to every one that he is a fool.

And foolish behavior is that of a child – figuratively speaking. Reader, please take note: A grown person's mind can still be that of a child engaging in foolishness and not that of an adult, which requires the practice of wisdom.

Proverbs 22:15
Foolishness is bound in the heart of a child; but the rod of correction shall drive it far from him

The rod of correction for ignorance and foolishness is knowledge, understanding, and wisdom.

1 Peter 2:15
For so is the will of God, that with well doing ye may put to silence the ignorance of foolish men.

In the world of young people, I have witnessed ignorance being the pathogen and the disease. In essence, ignorance begets ignorance. One youth says or acts it; the other youth actively and passively accepts it and thus, spreads the ignorance.

Isaiah 56:10
His watchmen are blind: they are all ignorant, they are all dumb dogs, they cannot bark; sleeping, lying down, loving to slumber.

Hebrews 5:2
Who can have compassion on the ignorant, and on them that are out of the way; for that he himself also is compassed with infirmity

I must say to the youths, do not follow ignorance.

> 1 Corinthians 14:38
> But if any man be ignorant, let him be ignorant.

Let's continue.

In the youth's world, too often ignorance is the prelude to sex, violence, death, etc.

Sex – *Everyone's doing it, no big deal?*
This type of ignorant behavior has contributed to sexually transmitted infections/diseases, unwanted pregnancies, single parent households, abortions, poverty, etc. Therefore, the casualness of having sex is devastating to families.

As a former teacher of Anatomy and Physiology, I introduced the topic of sex by saying, *"Unfortunately, we teach sex education as a public health issue instead of discussing the devastating consequences (previously listed). In addition, public education does not discuss how one's psyche and self esteem are affected by the number of non-committal sexual encounters. From my experience, young females (ages 13-25) are especially distressed and depressed when realizing the extreme number of sexual acts in which they have engaged and have not resulted in a commitment or a proposal.*

The act of engaging in sex requires communication and commitment. To be quite honest, many married couples lack communication and commitment. Therefore, many married couples should not be having sex."

Real Story 24
After lecturing on Sexually Transmitted diseases, a student approached me. The student asked many specific questions about symptoms and effects. The student said, "I've been having a discharge. It's green and smelly." I asked, "How come you didn't go to your parents?" She said, "My mom is mad at me. She found out that I've been having sex."

I immediately walked her to the school nurse and contacted her mother. The mother was furious. Next, the student said, "I've had

the discharge for several weeks."
      Several days later, the student told me how grateful she was. The student stated she had an STD.

It is worth noting that the young lady was a single parent. The young lady's parents were providing for and taking care of their grandchild so the girl could finish high school.

Obvious question:

Do you think the young lady communicated with her sexual partner about her disease?

Think.

When I teach about sex, the pictures I show not only elicit shock and *'gross out-ness'* but great dialog, even a monolog from me. I love to act out the expressions on the faces of students when asked questions like:

   1. If you are engaging in sex, would you tell your partner about having an infection or disease?

   2. Do you have the type of commitment and communication with your sex partner where by you will tell your partner or your partner will tell you about STIs/STDs contracted?

   3. Everyone you have sex with has the potential of being the mother or father of your child. Would your sex partner live up to the commitment of taking care of your child? Are you ready to take care of a child?

   4. If your previous sex partner from 2 years ago found out that he/she has contracted HPV or HIV or has Herpes or AIDS, do you think he/she would contact you to let you know?

   5. What about if you contracted HPV or HIV or have Herpes or AIDS, would you contact your former partner(s) to let him/her know?

6. What if the girl you had sex with a few years ago tells you, *'you are the father of her child.'* Would you want to be the father? Better yet, have you grown from being involved with that type of person?

7. Let's say you are married or involved with the person you plan to spend your life with and an old sex partner tells you he/she is dying from AIDS, and you need to get tested. You get tested and find out you have AIDS, would you tell your significant other? If so, how?

8. Let's say you find out that you are the father of a child. You go and visit the mother of your child and find out that they are living a dire situation. You are 19. Would you work to help get them out of the situation or would you say, "I can't do for myself, how can I help them, I can't."

Let's examine what things are real in our society.

After the party, I mean sex, is over, the girl is pregnant, the emotional relationship never existed and the commitment does not manifest. The girl get's an abortion; she is not committed to the life of an unborn child.

After the fun, I mean sex, is over, the girl is pregnant, the baby is born, and the father exits. This leads to another fatherless child.

After the relationship, I mean sex, is over, sexually transmitted infections and diseases are passed from one person to another and everyone is SILENT.

After the attraction, I mean sex, is over, the girl is pregnant, the emotional relationship never existed and the commitment does not manifest. The child is born. The mother hopes everything will be alright.

After the sex is over...
one HOPES one's not pregnant
one HOPES not to get an infection/disease
one HOPES that one will be loved
one HOPES that one does/will get married
one HOPES that one's child will not be fatherless
one HOPES that everything will be all right
one HOPES, etc...

However, HOPE is not a plan.

Overcoming Violence
Recently, I spoke with a group of students discussing violence in America. They indicated that they could not get around it, and fights occur in every school. Without intention, the group of three students increased to seven. The students were disclosing their perceptions of society.
    Let me tell you how the conversation began. I overheard some students discussing fighting. One student was talking about what he would have to do if a particular student decided to fight him. This was a golden moment. It was my cue to intervene, and I did.

Austin: What do you think the other person will do? Better yet, can I give an example?

Student: Yes.

Austin: If you were teasing another student, what do you think the other student would do?
(*Several answers were given in this order: 1. get mad, 2. fight me, 3. tease me, 4. hurt me, and 5. kill me. I commented on how interesting that the worst scenario was given last.*)

Austin: Suppose he kills you first? (*Students shrugged their shoulders*). You can't control a person's reaction. That student may just decide to kill you. Most students think a person will react the same way they would, and that's not always the case.

You can't control people nor can you actualize how they will respond.

Student: Yes, I understand, but violence is everywhere. You have to defend yourself.

Austin: Ok. Let's say violence is everywhere – for the moment. Let's say you live to be at least 75 years of age. You graduate at 18 years of age. You are left with 57 years to do things your way, and the chances are slim that you will ever see any of these students again. From my own personal experience, out of a high school graduating class of four hundred students, I've only associated with four students since high school. Trust me; you're not going to see most of these students ever again.

Student: Well, we do try to avoid fights. I mostly fight for family, and family is important.

Austin: True. Family is important.
(At this point, I drew a diagram with two sides and a barrier in between.)

Here's where you are.
(I pointed to the side of the diagram I had labeled <u>high school</u>.)

This is where you will be after high school.
(Pointing to the other side... I had labeled the following terms on this side: <u>college</u>, <u>job</u>, <u>profession</u>, <u>career</u>, and <u>family</u>.)

You have to see beyond high school, and determine how what you do over here (pointing to side 1) will affect you over here (pointing towards side 2).

(I continued pointing, with this back and forth action, while discussing how you must determine what you need to do over here to help you get over there. I could see it in their eyes. They were thinking.)

Austin Cont.: The chances are greater that you will never see these kids again. Don't make choices that could wreck the next 57 years.

Student: What do you want me to do? Walk away?

Austin: If necessary, move or go to another school.

Student: Then, they'll call you a punk, and this is a good school. A lot of rich students go here.

Austin: Yes, they may call you a punk. However, the chances are greater that you will never see them again, and there are more overextended students than rich students.

Students: Yes. You're right.

Austin: Do you believe that just as violence can occur anywhere, good can occur anywhere?
(A short pause occurred.)

Students: Yes.

Austin: How many of you travel and are exposed to the good in society?

Student: Man, my parents work all the time.

Austin: Well, I really want you to find preventable solutions like choosing your friends more wisely, stop butting into other folks business, learn to keep your mouth shut sometimes, focus on getting to the other side – over the barrier, and stop criticizing and putting people down. If you do these things, I guarantee you will get into fewer confrontations. (At that point, one of the students sat straight up.) Plus, expose yourself to the good in society. Travel, meet new people, and try new things.

Your words and actions are powerful. You can build empires, manifest dreams, and create friends with your words, or you can tear people down and start wars. The choice is yours. The world is yours.

Statistic 1:
According to the Center for Disease Control, homicide is the second cause of death for young people 15-to-24 years of age and the fifth cause of death for young people 10-to-14 years of age.

Real Story 25
Many students drive to school daily. A student receives a learner's permit at 15 1/2 years of age and a license at age 16. A month later, the student gets a car. One morning, the student is running late for school. The student crashes and dies in a car accident. It is concluded that the student was driving at a high rate of speed.

Statistic 2:
The Center for Disease Control (CDC) lists automobile accidents as the number one cause of teen deaths. On average, one teen death occurs every 91 minutes.

Factors contributing to teen vehicle crashes include inexperience, low rates of seat belt use, alcohol and text messaging.

Getting to adult behavior
Step 1: One must understand that adult behavior is the behavior of the wise. Therefore one must be taught wisdom and one must learn wisdom.

The rod of correction in Proverbs 22:15 results in giving wisdom through teaching, learning and demonstrations of knowledge, understanding, and wisdom.

> *Proverbs 29:15*
> *The rod and reproof give <u>wisdom</u>: but a child left to himself bringeth his mother to shame.*

Step 2: One must seek and get knowledge, understanding and wisdom

> *Proverbs 4:7*
> *Wisdom is the principal thing; therefore get wisdom: and*

with all thy getting get understanding.

Proverbs 14:6
A scorner seeketh wisdom, and findeth it not: but knowledge is easy unto him that understandeth.

Proverbs 18:1
Through desire a man, having separated himself, seeketh and intermeddleth with all wisdom.

Ecclesiastes 1:13
And I gave my heart to seek and search out by wisdom concerning all things that are done under heaven: this sore travail hath God given to the sons of man to be exercised therewith

Proverbs 15:14
The heart of him that hath understanding seeketh knowledge: but the mouth of fools feedeth on foolishness

Step 3: One must recognize ignorance and foolishness. And, distinguish those things from knowledge, understanding, and wisdom.

Ecclesiastes 7:25
I applied mine heart to know, and to search, and to seek out wisdom, and the reason of things, and to know the wickedness of folly, even of foolishness and madness:

Step 4: One must demonstrate knowledge, understanding, and wisdom to get to Adult behavior.

1 Peter 2:15
For so is the will of God, that with well doing ye may put to silence the ignorance of foolish men:

1 Corinthians 13:11
When I was a child, I spake as a child, I understood as a

child, I thought as a child: but when I became a man, I put away childish things

Today is preparation for tomorrow
Again, hope is not a plan.

Today's child is tomorrow's adult. Today, you must make steps towards tomorrow.

How are you preparing for tomorrow, today?

If you need a scholarship for college, are you studying, are maintaining a B+ average or above, and do you have a high SAT score?

Time spent volunteering, skill building, engaging in enrichment programs, establishing goal related time lines, and creating step-by-step guides are things you can do today to earn the work experience and the scholarship needed for tomorrow.

My husband disclosed to me that he envisioned his family setting as being to the one shown on the *'Leave it to Beaver'* show. He grew up without a father and dreamed of the day he could be a father. If you have ever seen or get to see the show, you will notice the character of the Father as being one of patience and understanding. Needless to say, he has the patience of JOB, when it comes to parenting; his listening skills are amazing.

LOL moment
During our first few holidays together, the strangest thing would occur. He would stare at me as I made my pies from scratch. Later I learned that the apron I wore represented part of his manifested vision.

What is your ideal mate? Are you exhibiting the characteristics needed to attract your desired person? Do you have a plan for your success; do you have a plan for the success of your family?

Yin-Yang

'*Yin-yang*' and '*conflict-ease*' are metaphors that symbolize ideas about negative-positive energy cycles. These cycles reflect the need to prepare for success. During times of yang/ease (positive energy flow) one must prepare for yin/conflict (negative energy flow). Engaging in this strategy allows one to be prepared during the most difficult times of his/her life, and to maneuver through such times successfully.

Preparations for college, career, family, buying a home, entrepreneurship, and success start today. Steps towards future financial stability should be taken today. Read books that teach you how to save and build wealth. Some books start with simple saving methods, such as saving fifteen dollars a week.

I do not believe in creating chaos. Life will present challenges of its own. There is no need to create drama. The goal is to be ready for the challenges, the unforeseen circumstances, the accidents and the crises that come in life.

The '*yin and the yang*', as well as the '*conflict and ease*' cycles remind us that life is not unbearable when we plan through the use of knowledge, wisdom, and understanding. Therefore, this is a concept I strongly recommend that you implement in your life.

> *1 Corinthians 12:1*
> *Now concerning spiritual gifts, brethren, I would not have you ignorant.*

Ignorant Behavior is <u>not</u> Adult Behavior.

Life Lesson 6
Forgive, Trust, and Be Patient

In this life lesson, we are asking you to forgive those who trespass against you, trust in God to deliver his promise when you follow thee, and be patient as God's promise manifests.

Therefore, life lesson 6 is to forgive, trust and be patient.

'The Lord's Prayer' and the '23rd Psalm' are two of the most repeated scriptures from the bible. Every day, many say these scriptures in faith that if we forgive and trust, God will deliver his promise. We just need to be patient.

The Lord's Prayer:

> Matthew 6
> ^{9}...Our Father which art in heaven, Hallowed be thy name.
> ^{10}Thy kingdom come, Thy will be done in earth, as it is in heaven.
> ^{11}Give us this day our daily bread.
> ^{12}And forgive us our debts, as we forgive our debtors.
> ^{13}And lead us not into temptation, but deliver us from evil: For thine is the kingdom, and the power, and the glory, for ever. Amen.

The 23rd Psalm:

> Psalm 23
> ¹The LORD is my shepherd; I shall not want.
> ²He maketh me to lie down in green pastures: he leadeth me beside the still waters.
> ³He restoreth my soul: he leadeth me in the paths of righteousness for his name's sake.
> ⁴Yea, though I walk through the valley of the shadow of death, I will fear no evil: for thou art with me; thy rod and thy staff they comfort me.
> ⁵Thou preparest a table before me in the presence of mine enemies: thou anointest my head with oil; my cup runneth over.
> ⁶Surely goodness and mercy shall follow me all the days of my life: and I will dwell in the house of the LORD for ever.

Again, our six life lesson is **'You must forgive, trust and be patient'**.

FORGIVE...

> Matthew 6:14
> For if ye forgive men their trespasses, your heavenly Father will also forgive you:

When one forgives, one is releasing limiting thoughts such as resentment and disappointment. In holding on to anger and frustration, which generally accompany unforgiveness, one's positive creative life enhancing energy is diminished. Instead, one is using their energy to proliferate fear, anger, and frustration. In order to move forward, i.e. progress in life, you must forgive. Thus, allowing your spirit to be free and not confined by the emotions of the body.

This is why our six life lesson embodies forgiveness.

In **Luke 23:34**, Jesus said, **"Father, forgive them for they know not what they do."** Luke 23:24 is such a powerful statement of wisdom, especially the part, *'for they know not what they do'*. When people trespass against you or commit a sin against you, they do not know that the penalty is greater on them, then you.

Why?

First, let us set the context for the answer. There are two types of people who will trespass against you: those who know better and those who do not. Have you ever heard of the cliché, *'If they knew better, they will do better'*? As you go through life, you will learn that many people who offend us don't know they did it. They have no clue. Therefore, while you are busy being angry and upset, they have gone on about their business and about their life.

Therefore, when people trespass against you, you may want to speak with them to find out if they knew that their actions were offensive. I often tell students, *'while you're upset, the other person may be at Disney World having a great time.'*

On the other hand, when people know they have offended you, they may not know that they are stopping their blessing(s). Don't take it personally. They are using their energy to create a world of chaos around them, negative energy-zapping *'sucking the rewards out of life'* chaos. Many people, who knowingly offend others, will irritate, annoy and offend again and again at the expense of them transgressing against self and God.

How are they transgressing against God?

Reason #1: You can't say you love God and not show Agape' love towards your follow man.

> 1 John 4:7
> *Beloved, let us love one another: for love is of God; and every one that loveth is born of God, and knoweth God.*
>
> 1 John 4:19-21
> *We love him, because he first loved us.*
> *If a man say, I love God, and hateth his brother, he is a liar: for he that loveth not his brother whom he hath seen, how can*

> he love God whom he hath not seen?
> And this commandment have we from him, That he who loveth God love his brother also.

Reason #2: When one is so embedded in trespassing against others, one is letting the Body rule self and not God's Spirit within guide self.

Remember:
> James 2:26
> For as the body without the spirit is dead…

Generally speaking, we want the person, who has trespassed against us, to make us whole. We say, "*They owe us. They did me wrong. I will never forget what they did*".

Yes, the person did you wrong. Yes, you have been hurt or harmed by what the person did to you. Yes, the trespass was irresponsible and the person should be held accountable. Yes, the trespass warrants an apology or compensation. Yes! Yes! Yes! Yes, you are right. And, yes you must forgive.

When you forgive, you are releasing all negative thoughts associated with the trespass, the sin and the offense against you. You are releasing doubt, anger, frustration, hate, distrust, etc. When you forgive, you release those thoughts and the limits they have on you.

Real Story 26
I came across a young man who wasn't taking care of his children. His mother aired to me, he wasn't active in their lives. The mother really believed that her son did not know how-to be involved because his father was not in his life.

I told the young man there is nothing wrong with reading books on how to father. You can start by watching re-runs of 'The Cosby Show', 'Leave it to Beaver', and '7th Heaven'. He laughed.

I concluded with, "He, who gets the kids, gets the blessings." I stated to him, "I never have known any man to live a blessed life who didn't take care of his child. I think there's something Spiritual about that."

Continuing...

How many males are out-of-touch with their children or angry and bitter that there wasn't a father around?

I can give you an answer from experience, *'a lot'*.

I come in contact with many young people from age 4 to 40; young people who tell me or show me how angry they are because their fathers are not in their lives. Some share the mistakes they have made; they believe these mistakes occurred because their fathers were absent and they lacked a father's guidance, wisdom, and involvement. Their fathers weren't there to teach them; so, they are angry. Some even pass this anger on to their child. I have heard many say, *"My father wasn't there for me, so why should I be there for my child."* For some young men, there is nothing they feel need to be said; they just are not around their child.

Do you think if a person knew the penalty for abandoning one's child they would do it?

Even when we don't see a person being held liable for their offense(s), does not mean they aren't being held accountable.

Real Story 27
A young lady was raped. During the trial, the man was found not guilty. The woman was very angry. After she told me her story, I asked about the perpetrated. She stated that he was homeless, basically; he had no known family and no known support system.

I said to her, "Wow, prison would have been a good thing for him. He would have had three meals a day, access to medical treatment, and a roof over his head." She quickly and for a very short moment, generated a controlled smile. I continued by saying, "You know, God has a way of holding people more accountable than man could ever do."

> Luke 23: 34
> Then Jesus said, Father, forgive them for they know not what they do.

In essence, when we forgive, we no-longer hold onto the ignorance of others who have offended. We release them and their ignorance of not understanding...

A person who is allowing GOD to lead them and uses wisdom in attempts not to offend is blessed; he receives blessings.

> Luke 7:23
> And blessed is he, whosoever shall not be offended in me

It is my belief that if one who offends others knew one was shutting off blessings, one would not offend. Therefore, I believe that one offends because one does not know...

> Luke 23: 34
> ...for they know not what they do.

Therefore, *Forgive*.

TRUST...

> Proverbs 3:5
> Trust in the LORD with all thine heart; and lean not unto thine own understanding.

Right now, I am thinking about how many young people are going to understand what very few grown people do; how many young people are not going to be swayed by their own understanding? This is what I am thinking, and this is what makes what I do so unique.

As with every book I write, I have to write from Spirit. The words have to come from the God spirit inside of me to connect to the God spirit inside of you. I cannot resort to the body of emotions or change how Spirit wants me to write.

When we say trust in the Lord, we include the act of believing the Lord. I once heard a Minister say, "*Many trust in Jesus, but many don't believe Jesus.*" We can easily substitute Jesus for God... '*Many trust in God, but many don't believe God.*'

This is why our six life lesson embodies trust.

Let us be honest. We know *Trusting in God* is not an easy thing to do. However, we do want to trust God and believe in God because of the '*Promise*'. Generally, but not always, when people refer to the '*Promise*' we are referencing the *Promise* God made to Abraham in Genesis 22.

> *Genesis 22: 17-18*
> *That in blessing I will bless thee, and in multiplying I will multiply thy seed as the stars of the heaven, and as the sand which is upon the sea shore; and thy seed shall possess the gate of his enemies;*
> *And in thy seed shall all the nations of the earth be blessed; because thou has obeyed my voice*

Here's a disclaimer: Based on tradition, religion and/or culture, the promise(s) may be different. Nonetheless, there is a shared universal belief, among people who believe in God, which is 'If we trust in God, he will keep the promise(s).'

Real Story 28
A ritual, during my college years, was to get together with friends on Friday nights and watch Miami Vice and there was alcohol involved. Next, we would crash (go to sleep), wake up and go home.
One particular Friday evening, I let a friend use my car to go to a party. I told him to drop me off at the house where this practice took place. We watched Miami Vice as usually. Played cards and crashed. However, this evening was different. I awoke to someone probing me, but there was no-one there. The feeling was so strong, and I quickly realize it was Spirit telling me to 'get up and get out'. I set up and quickly recognized there was no one around me. This was odd.
Still somewhat incoherent, I remember hearing noises from a

bedroom. I went to see what was going on. When I open the door, people were passing around a glass cylinder connected to a flask using a blow torch.

Next, the Force I knew was Spirit had taken command of me. All I could do was obey, and I did. I got my belonging and was out. I walked over a mile to my car, got in it, went to sleep and waited for the party to end. When my friend saw that I was in the car he asked what happened. I told him. He stated, "They were probably freebasing and I was lucky I left". I knew I wasn't lucky, I was blessed.

A lot of that type of Spirit moving activity happened during my young days, especially during college. I was too young and foolish to really know what was happening. When I became a parent, I realized it was all about the covenant my parents had with GOD, especially my mother. I could read the agreement on her face and see it in her eyes.

> 2 Chronicles 15:12
> And they entered into a covenant to seek the LORD God of their fathers with all their heart and with all their soul;

> 2 Samuel 22:3
> The God of my rock; in him will I trust: he is my shield, and the horn of my salvation, my high tower, and my refuge, my saviour; thou savest me from violence.

> Deuteronomy 30:19
> I call heaven and earth to record this day against you, that I have set before you life and death, blessing and cursing: therefore choose life, that both thou and thy seed may live

> Psalms 115: 11
> Ye that fear the Lord, trust in the Lord: he is their help and shield.

Ok, back to Abraham. You may be asking, 'What did Abraham do to deserve this Blessing?'

The answer, **he sacrificed**. Abraham trusted God with all his heart and leaned not unto his own understanding, and because of this, his seeds/children and children's children (for generations to come) will be blessed and receive the promise.

Sounds good, doesn't it?

Well it is. But... and there is a BUT- a BIG **BUT. YOU MUST HAVE FAITH!!!**

> *Romans 4:13*
> *For the promise, that he should be the heir of the world, was not to Abraham, or to his seed, through the law, but through the righteousness of faith*
>
> *Hebrews 11:17*
> *By faith Abraham, when he was tried, offered up Isaac...*
>
> *Galatians 3:14*
> *That the blessing of Abraham might come on the Gentiles through Jesus Christ; that we might receive the promise of the Spirit through faith.*
>
> *Hebrews 6:12*
> *That ye be not slothful, but followers of them who through faith and patience inherit the promises.*

You see, Abraham had faith in GOD and that is why he was able to obey God.

Do you have Faith?

Are you able to obey and follow the God spirit existing inside of you?

One reason why many people are not receiving the *Blessings of Abraham* or whatever promises they believe God has made to them is because of their inability to follow GOD.

Remember, the Blessing already has been fulfilled. *How...*you may ask. Here's an analogy. I am a mother and I bake my child's favorite cake. It's just sitting there. There it sits, on the counter, just waiting for my child to finish his dinner; that is all I requested.

What has GOD requested of you?

The answer, simply put, is...*Have Faith*, which means believe in me- I am your GOD...and *Follow Me*, which means let me guide you; listen to Spirit... I have placed my Spirit in you...I am always with you.

> *Acts 17:24*
> *God that made the world and all things therein, seeing that he is Lord of heaven and earth, dwelleth not in temples made with hands*

> *1 Corinthians 3:16*
> *Know ye not that ye are the temple of God, and that the Spirit of God dwelleth in you?*

> *Romans 8:9*
> *But ye are not in the flesh, but in the Spirit, if so be that the Spirit of God dwell in you. Now if any man have not the Spirit of Christ, he is none of his*

> *1 John 3:24*
> *And he that keepeth his commandments dwelleth in him, and he in him. And hereby we know that he abideth in us, by the Spirit which he hath given us.*

> *Matthew 28:20*
> *Teaching them to observe all things whatsoever I have commanded you: and, lo, I am with you always, even unto the end of the world. Amen.*

The first twelve verses of Psalm 139 beautifully and compassionately states GOD's omniscience and omnipresence.

YOU MUST FORGIVE, TRUST, AND BE PATIENT

Psalm 139

¹O lord, thou hast searched me, and known me.

²Thou knowest my downsitting and mine uprising, thou understand dest my thought afar off.

³Thou compassest my path and my lying down, and art acquainted with all my ways.

⁴For there is not a word in my tongue, but, lo, O LORD, thou knowest it altogether.

⁵Thou hast beset me behind and before, and laid thine hand upon me.

⁶Such knowledge is too wonderful for me; it is high, I cannot attain unto it.

⁷Whither shall I go from thy spirit? or whither shall I flee from thy presence?

⁸If I ascend up into heaven, thou art there: if I make my bed in hell, behold, thou art there.

⁹If I take the wings of the morning, and dwell in the uttermost parts of the sea;

¹⁰Even there shall thy hand lead me, and thy right hand shall hold me.

¹¹If I say, Surely the darkness shall cover me; even the night shall be light about me.

¹²Yea, the darkness hideth not from thee; but the night shineth as the day: the darkness and the light are both alike to thee.

Continuing...

Keep in mind, the *Faith* you have requires work (the following of God's Spirit).

Deuteronomy 1:11

(The LORD God of your fathers make you a thousand times so many more as ye are, and bless you, as he hath promised you!)

> *Deuteronomy 15:6*
> *For the LORD thy God blesseth thee, as he promised thee: and thou shalt lend unto many nations, but thou shalt not borrow; and thou shalt reign over many nations, but they shall not reign over thee.*

I remember when I was a child. My mother would tell me she was going to bake a cake and I would have to eat my dinner. There were times when I ate my dinner before she ever started baking the cake. That was the *Faith* of a child. Not only did I believe in my mother's existence, which was easy because I could see her, I believed her.

Question: *Does the blind child have more faith?*

The blind child must believe beyond sight in his mother's existence and believe her.

As we grow and mature, many are under the constraints of what they can see. We even have a saying, 'When I see it, I will believe it.' I understand the saying and how it should be used – with man, not with GOD.

> *1 Corinthians 2:5*
> *That your faith should not stand in the wisdom of men, but in the power of God.*

My reality from my life experiences acknowledges many people who believe in God. However, I find that their faith waiver from time to time. They just are not sure if the blessing (ex. cake) is there or will be there after they work (follow Spirit) their faith; nevertheless, it is.

> *Ruth 2:12*
> *The LORD recompense thy work, and a full reward be given thee of the LORD God of Israel, under whose wings thou art come to trust.*

Lack of Trust...Blaming Others

Reader, one reason for writing this book is to enlighten you about what I have witnessed, learned, and experienced; I want you to live long days.

As you grow in your spirituality, you will begin to notice how people blame others for their misfortunes, non-manifestations of their dreams and unfulfillment of God's promise. In some religions, cultures and traditions, Satan, the Devil and the enemy quite often are blamed for a person's lack of trust in God, not believing God and therefore, not listening to GOD.

Whether you believe in Satan, the Devil, the enemy or some other entity opposite of GOD is not for me to question. I only hope that in your life, if things go awry, you are able to ponder on the cause and your thinking in an effort to come away with a true understanding of how the result(s) manifested/came into being.

Remember, **GOD is Omnipotent**- All Powerful

> *Matthew 12:28*
> *But if I cast out devils by the Spirit of God, then the kingdom of God is come unto you.*

> *Ephesians 6:11*
> *Put on the whole armour of God, that ye may be able to stand against the wiles of the devil.*

> *James 4:7*
> *Submit yourselves therefore to God. Resist the devil, and he will flee from you.*

> *Matthew 4:10*
> *Then saith Jesus unto him, Get thee hence, Satan: for it is written, Thou shalt worship the Lord thy God, and him only shalt thou serve.*

> *Acts 26:18*
> *To open their eyes, and to turn them from darkness to light,*

and from the power of Satan unto God, that they may receive forgiveness of sins, and inheritance among them which are sanctified by faith that is in me.

Romans 16:20
And the God of peace shall bruise Satan under your feet shortly. The grace of our Lord Jesus Christ be with you. Amen.

Judges 16:24
And when the people saw him, they praised their god: for they said, Our god hath delivered into our hands our enemy, and the destroyer of our country, which slew many of us.

Deuteronomy 33:27
The eternal God is thy refuge, and underneath are the everlasting arms: and he shall thrust out the enemy from before thee; and shall say, Destroy them

Ezekiel 36:2
Thus saith the Lord GOD; Because the enemy hath said against you, Aha, even the ancient high places are ours in possession:

The devil, satan, the enemy or others have no Power over the All Powerful Omnipotent GOD; they have no power over the GOD Spirit inside of you. And, they have no power over you when you follow GOD.

Lack of Trust...Blaming Generational Curses
Family lifestyles are passed down from generation to generation. This is why so-called curses appear to exist. Simply put, stop the lifestyle and you stop the behavior. Stop the behavior and you stop the negative consequence. The GOD spirit inside of me wants to let you know, GOD is not interested in giving you an everlasting state of perpetual hell because of what your parents have done.

2 Chronicles 25:4
But he slew not their children, but did as it is written in the

law in the book of Moses, where the LORD commanded, saying, The fathers shall not die for the children, neither shall the children die for the fathers, but every man shall die for his own sin.

Real Story 29
One condition, which seems to plague our family from generation to generation, is divorce. Therefore, prior to getting married, I studied our family history, spoke with couples who had been married for more than 30+ years, read books, etc. So far, the length of my marriage is longer than those of my parents and their parents.

When generations of a family appear to be blessed, we perceive their tradition and culture in a state of respect for God, tuning in to God, seeking and exhibiting knowledge, wisdom, and understanding, listening to God's Spirit and having faith.

However, don't confuse being blessed with being wealthy. Being blessed means being whole – one's spiritual, mental, emotional and physical needs are abundantly met.

When generations of a family appear to be in constant turmoil, we deemed them as being cursed. Violence, ill-health, constantly mental, emotional and physical needs are not met and there is a lack of understanding and demonstration of adhering to God's guidance in their lives.

> *Deuteronomy 30:19*
> *...that I have set before you life and death, blessing and cursing: therefore choose life, that both thou and thy seed may live*

Lack of Trust...Not believing God's promise of 'Power of the Tongue'...
In an earlier chapter, we discussed GOD's creations possessing his Spirit and having <u>Power</u>, including his creation of man. YOU.

> Proverbs 18:21
> Death and life are in the power of the tongue: and they that love it shall eat the fruit thereof.

We cannot forget this. Man has the power to create and manifest. As such, many overlook their power being a factor in the materialization of undesirable conditions expressed in their lives and the prevention of obtainable blessings.

Question: *What do you think would have happened if the child informed the mother that he wasn't going to eat his dinner or I don't want the cake?*

Answer: *He would have used his power to create the negative result of blocking his blessing.*

Real Story 30
Our organization was under contract on an office space being underutilized. My Spirit told me that it was time to relinquish the office. I no longer had a vision to be there. When I entered the office, I could feel conflict in my Soul. However, I didn't know what to do. There was no legal way to terminate the agreement.

I would air to my husband, "We need to get out of this lease." I even stated several times to a Board Member how it would be great if we could be relieved of the financial obligation. Within a few weeks, the leasing company breached the contract allowing us to be released from the agreement.

I didn't do anything other than speak the words. Words have power, and my words brought death to that situation.

> John 15:7
> If ye abide in me, and my words abide in you, ye shall ask what ye will, and it shall be done unto you.

Real Story 30
In 2001 after being asked by parents if their was a book I could recom-

mend, I told the parents I would write them a book because I couldn't find one I could suggest. I tried to write the book, but quickly got writer's block.

Fast forward to 2003: One month prior to being offered an Administrative position, I briefly passed by my former principal in the School District's Administrative offices. He was looking for teachers and inquired as to what I was doing. I told him I was interested in an Administrative position.

Within a month, several extraordinary events occurred while I was on vocation in Hawaii. Upon my returned, I was offered an Administrative position in an Alternative School. The experiences at the Alternative school broke the writer's block I had in trying to complete my first book.

Just before completing my tenure at the school, God's Spirit spoke to me and told me I would not be there long. The next day, my assignment at the school was over. I heard Spirit speak again saying, "Go write my book". I went home, took out the book I had started two years earlier, and for the first time saw every chapter. The experience from that Administrative position created the first and last chapters in the book; both chapters are about love – the most powerful force in the Universe (originating with God's love for us and how he created us).

That book is titled, **From Parent to Power**. When people find out I wrote the book they have read, their powerful words of appreciation fill my heart as they express their enlightenment.

I spoke the words to bring my book into being. The All Knowing Omniscient GOD knew what was going to happen with my Administrative assignment from Alpha to Omega. From the beginning to the end, GOD ordered my steps and I went with the flow.

Unfortunately, there were blessings I have blocked and negative situations I have created in my life. Not many, but enough for me to have taken the time to recondition my mouth and heart to reflect not only what I want in life, but to be positively aligned with the God spirit that resides in me.

Psalm 19:14
Let the words of my mouth, and the meditation of my heart,

be acceptable in thy sight, O LORD, my strength, and my redeemer.

Overall
God is Omniscience, all-knowing, Omnipresence, present everywhere, and Omnipotent, all-powerful. There is no greater force in the Universe other than GOD. Regardless of your circumstances and your beliefs, not only Trust in GOD, but Trust GOD.

Proverbs 3:5
Trust in the LORD with all thine heart; and lean not unto thine own understanding.

PATIENCE...
Hebrews 10:36
For ye have need of patience, that, after ye have done the will of God, ye might receive the promise

Patience is a cultivation period. The cultivation period begins after you've completed your GOD given assignment and ends with the obtainment of your blessings. During cultivation, preparation is taking place and improvements are being made to foster viability – success. Webster defines patience as willingness/ability to bear calmly without complaints.

I heard people refer to this period as the trial period. I believe such a reference lacks full understanding of what is going on – cultivation. Cultivation embodies the person (receiving the blessing), the blessing and the environment going through a state of preparation and improvements. Think of a farmer, who plants tomato seeds. *Will the seeds instantly sprout? Is the environment 100% conducive for bringing forth tomatoes?* The answer to both is 'No'. Both processes require a period of cultivation.

Therefore, our emphasis on patience must include the understanding of who and what are being cultivated to bring forth good fruit.

> *Luke 8:15*
> *But that on the good ground are they, which in an honest and good heart, having heard the word, keep it, and bring forth fruit with patience.*

This is why our six life lesson embodies patience.

Here's what I have witnessed. When negative events, actions and reactions such as pain, suffering, sadness, etc. concurrently exist along side of the cultivation period, words like trial, temptation, and tribulation are often used. When positive events, actions, and reactions parallel the cultivation period, hopefulness, faithfulness and patience are spoken.

In either case...

After you have done the will of GOD, follow GOD's Spirit within you and hope for success, you must have patience...

> *Romans 8:25*
> *But if we hope for that we see not, then do we with patience wait for it.*

After you have done the will of GOD, follow GOD's Spirit within you and there is the appearance of trials and tribulations, you must have patience...

> *Romans 5:3*
> *And not only so, but we glory in tribulations also: knowing that tribulation worketh patience;*

After you have done the will of GOD, follow GOD's Spirit within you and your self-constraint is tested or in the young people's world: you want to 'go off', you must elicit temperance; you must have patience...

> *2 Peter 1:4-8*
> *Whereby are given unto us exceeding great and precious*

promises: that by these ye might be partakers of the divine nature, having escaped the corruption that is in the world through lust.

And beside this, giving all diligence, add to your faith virtue; and to virtue knowledge;

And to knowledge temperance; and to temperance patience; and to patience godliness

And to godliness brotherly kindness; and to brotherly kindness charity.

For if these things be in you, and abound, they make you that ye shall neither be barren nor unfruitful in the knowledge of our Lord Jesus Christ.

Job
Job, pronounced Jōb not jŏb (work, duty, responsibility), is most closely associate with patience.

James 5:11
Behold, we count them happy which endure. Ye have heard of the patience of Job, and have seen the end of the Lord; that the Lord is very pitiful, and of tender mercy

Job listened and obeyed God; he was a righteous man.

Job 1:1
There was a man in the land of Uz, whose name was Job; and that man was perfect and upright, and one that feared God, and eschewed evil.

Job was very very blessed.

Job 1:2-3
And there were born unto him seven sons and three daughters.

His substance also was seven thousand sheep, and three thousand camels, and five hundred yoke of oxen, and five hundred she asses, and a very great household; so that this man was the greatest of all the men of the east

In addition, because of the covenant between Job and God, no ill could come to him.

> 2 Chronicles 15:12
> And they entered into a covenant to seek the LORD God of their fathers with all their heart and with all their soul;

> 2 Samuel 22:3
> The God of my rock; in him will I trust: he is my shield, and the horn of my salvation, my high tower, and my refuge, my saviour; thou savest me from violence.

Literally interpreting the Book of Job best describes the link between Job and patience. In such, God removes his protection from Job and allows Satan to bring upon Job a series of negative distressing events. God believes that during the trial and tribulation, Job will remain devoted to him and continue to honor him. Satan, on the other hand, believes Job will disapprove of God and curse him.

In Chapter 1, Job lost his servants, oxen, asses, sheep, camels and his children – all had perished.

> Job 1:13-19
> And there was a day when his sons and his daughters were eating and drinking wine in their eldest brother's house:
> And there came a messenger unto Job, and said, The oxen were plowing, and the asses feeding beside them:
> And the Sabeans fell upon them, and took them away; yea, they have slain the servants with the edge of the sword; and I only am escaped alone to tell thee.
> While he was yet speaking, there came also another, and said, The fire of God is fallen from heaven, and hath burned up the sheep, and the servants, and consumed them; and I only am escaped alone to tell thee.
> While he was yet speaking, there came also another, and

> said, The Chaldeans made out three bands, and fell upon the camels, and have carried them away, yea, and slain the servants with the edge of the sword; and I only am escaped alone to tell thee.
> While he was yet speaking, there came also another, and said, Thy sons and thy daughters were eating and drinking wine in their eldest brother's house:
> And, behold, there came a great wind from the wilderness, and smote the four corners of the house, and it fell upon the young men, and they are dead; and I only am escaped alone to tell thee.

After all this and in the midst of trials and tribulations **Job demonstrated patience**. Job worshipped and blessed God. He did not curse God.

> Job 1:20-22
> Then Job arose, and rent his mantle, and shaved his head, and fell down upon the ground, and worshipped,
> And said, Naked came I out of my mother's womb, and naked shall I return thither: the LORD gave, and the LORD hath taken away; blessed be the name of the LORD.
> In all this Job sinned not, nor charged God foolishly

In Chapter 2, when Job's skin was covered with boils and fell from its bone, **Job demonstrated patience**. He did not curse God.

> Job 2:7
> So went Satan forth from the presence of the LORD, and smote Job with sore boils from the sole of his foot unto his crown.

> Job 2:10
> ...In all this did not Job sin with his lips.

Read Story 31
A young man told me about his relationship with his father. He stated, "Throughout the years, every time I would ask my father for something

he claimed he did not have the money. Once, he called and told me he would buy whatever I wanted for Christmas. I did trust him to get what I wanted. And, he didn't get it. When I turned eighteen, he told me I was an adult and on my own."

As I listened to this young man, I sensed no animosity in his voice. I perceived this young man to have an understanding beyond his human circumstance. You could see the faith, hope, and patience he exhibited knowing things will get better.

> Romans 8:25
> But if we hope for that we see not, then do we with patience wait for it.

Let's return to Job.

In summary, during Job's trials and tribulations...

Job questions and asks 'Why me?'
Job questions his ability and capability to bear and stand in the mist of troubles.
Job pleads to be delivered from his ordeal and he asks for knowledge, wisdom, and understanding wherein he has erred.
Job loses hope that he will live.
Job divulges that what is occurring to him doesn't make sense.
Job declares that he will hold on to his righteousness.

However, Job does not denounce or curse God. In layman's terms, Job never states, 'I hate God', 'there is no God', or 'I don't believe in God.'

Because Job endured in his trial and tribulation and maintained his righteousness of honoring God he was blessed. The Lord gave Job twice as much as he had before.

> Job 42:12
> So the LORD blessed the latter end of Job more than his beginning: for he had fourteen thousand sheep, and

six thousand camels, and a thousand yoke of oxen, and a thousand she asses.

Job 42: 16-17
After this lived Job an hundred and forty years, and saw his sons, and his sons' sons, even four generations.
So Job died, being old and full of days.

Forgive, trust, and be patient.

Life Lesson 7
GOD has <u>not</u> forgotten YOU

Our seventh and final life lesson is *'God has <u>not</u> forgotten YOU'*.

When I started this book, I had the last chapter titled *'You can control your destiny'*. I wanted the youth and young adults to know they had the *Power* and *Authority* to direct their life's path regardless of their circumstances. Although that was my title, God had his title. And, it is *'God has not forgotten you'*. God's voice was clear; HE said, "From reading this book, they (the readers) will know they possess the power and authority to control their life. However, based on what some of them have gone through, they may not know that I have not forgotten them. And, that is what I truly want them to know - I have not forgotten them."

God's voice was loud and clear and HE wants me to tell you that HE has not forgotten you. Regardless of your circumstances, whether you were abandoned, rejected, molested, raped, abused, mistreated, or you had killed, aborted a child, or lost a loved one, etc., God wants you to know that he has not forgotten you, and HE is always present with you and for you.

Therefore, our seventh and final life lesson is *'GOD has <u>not</u> forgotten YOU'*.

Side note:
When God gave me this chapter, I thought about how this is an awesome assignment God has gifted to me. Why? God is constantly giving people task. So, why me? Well, I believe one factor is I see children, young people, adults, and parents who never have gotten over being abandoned, abused, rejected, emotionally mistreated, in physical mental pain, anguish, etc. And, the one missing component in the abuse, the abandonment, the adoption, the violence, etc., is that these individuals feel no-one loves them, they weren't loved enough nor were they unconditionally loved. Being unconditionally loved by someone wasn't part of their life and for that, GOD must have forgotten them.

In a nutshell, God presented this undertaking to me, and I accepted the job. However, as with every assignment GOD gives me, I tend to lag behind in the knowledge needed to definitively convey GOD's message. This requires patience and an open mind on my part as GOD reveals knowledge and understanding.

I've seen how people in pain create self destructive behavior and generational curses from their experiences. From suicide to passing this behavior onto their children. And, in some shape, form or fashion this negativity becomes the tone, tradition and culture in their life.

I am here to tell you, GOD HAS NOT FORGOTTEN YOU. HE LOVES YOU - ALWAYS HAS AND ALWAYS WILL.

Real Story 32
Born disabled and to alcoholic parents, a young man experienced being confined to a wheelchair and raised in an abusive household. Child Protective Services enters his life and he is removed from the home moving from one foster care home to another. Eventually, he is adopted.

Intelligent, very smart and talented, the now soon to be high school graduate doesn't think much about the future. He even airs that he does not believe in GOD.

When I was told about his story from someone very close to him, my first response was, "I understand why he feels that way." I briefly flashed back to my twenties when I claimed skepticism in God's existence. Full atheism failed to set in due to an inevitable confrontation requiring a resolution beyond self-control, i.e. a miracle, thus preventing my frustration from circumventing my God given common sense knowledge of God's existence.

In my thirties, I debated with a good friend about the existence of God. From my experience, I voiced that by default people attend church more out of an expectation, hoping God will remember to bless them, than out of a true worship of God.

Now, in my forties, I am a good messenger to tell you God has not forgotten you. HE's here for you. Just listen to him. And, learn the voice inside of you which speaks to you.

In an earlier chapter, we discussed the 23 Psalm, i.e. *The Lord is my shepherd....* Just as a flock of sheep must learn the voice of their shepherd, we must learn the voice of the Lord, our shepherd. In a society where impatience and expediency are the norms, one may forget that there is a Shepherd which speaks from within – a God who loves you and is there to guide you. Learn the voice of the Shepherd, Your God.

In a recent version of *'The Count of Monte Cristo'*, I heard one of the most profound statements – **'He believes in you'**. I have recounted the dialog below.

> (**Background**: Edmond Dantes, the man who will soon become The Count of Monte Cristo is imprisoned for a crime of murder, which he did not commit. While incarcerated, he meets Abbe Faria, better known as 'Priest', who will become Edmond's mentor. On Abbe Faria death bed, the following dialogue takes place.)
>
> **Abbe Faria:** "...Do not commit the crimes for which you now serve the sentence. God said vengeance is mines."
>
> **Edmond Dantes:** "I don't believe in God'
>
> **Abbe Faria:** "It doesn't matter. He believes in you."

Yes, God believes in YOU.

Your Purpose
Have you ever heard, *God has put you here for a purpose* or *you have a purpose in life*?

I have. I also know how not knowing your purpose and going through trials, tribulations, ups, and downs can make one's life unbearable, frustrating and depressing.

I truly believe there is a purpose for our life. However, I don't believe that everything you go through contributes to God's purpose, especially if you refuse to listen to Spirit. For example, in Real Story 28, I didn't have to listen to Spirit to tell me to get up and get out of that situation. I could very well have ignored Spirit and suffer the consequence, something I've done later in my life.

Real Story 33
Spirit spoke clearly within me; telling me to get out of an 'up and down chaotic' relationship. I stayed in that relationship for 2 additional years. When I determined my purpose in life, I recognized that the additional time spent in the relationship yielded no experience or lesson associate with or helpful to my purpose.

During Christmas, upon visiting family in Chicago, my brother gave me a book he wanted me to read titled, *'Life on the Other Side'* by Sylvia Browne. In the book, Browne speaks on how we come from the other side with a pre-planned purpose accompanied with an agenda beginning with who we choose for our parents. On the other side, when we are more in tune with God and our possibilities, Browne alludes to our writing of hearty overzealous goals for the life we soon will encounter on Earth.

My take on the book was a reaffirming that there is a purpose for our life. And, it presented the following challenge to me – if I am the one who wrote the script for my life, no matter how haughty the challenge, I must have believed I could accomplish it even through all the trials and tribulation, ups and downs, etc. More importantly, I recognize that I am well equip to discover and complete my purpose when I tune in to Spirit. Therefore, I will choose to revisit my inner spiritual voice and listen to it recognizing that my failure to listen to God's spirit and my choices may have been the cause for some of my negative experiences.

Despite appearances, not all circumstances, experiences and people are in your life to help you fulfill your purpose. Throughout your life, you will need to renew your soul by reconnecting with your Spirit and following Spirit's guidance on whom and what are the essentials to your purpose.

Renewing to Restore and Transform

I wrote a book titled *'From Parent to Power'*. The book helps parents with determining their purpose as a parent and governing their parenting to meet their parental purpose. The core purpose of parents is to guide the Spiritual child that was entrusted to them. At times parents forget their purpose, instead focusing on the child's position in the human world, which may be absent from a Spiritual connection with God or substituting rules in lieu of guidance, etc.

In the book, *'From Parent to Power'*, I write about how parents must renew themselves to get back to understanding their purpose; and, in life, one must renew one's self to get back to their purpose in life.

> Romans 12:2
> And be not conformed to this world: but be ye transformed by the renewing of your mind, that ye may prove what is that good, and acceptable, and perfect, will of God.

Renewing means *to restore to a former state, make new or as if new again*. Renewing allows one to reconnect with one's Spiritual part. Through the process of renewing, one is reminded to focus on their Spiritual Being as their guide and not the emotional whims when following the *body*.

> Psalm 23:3
> He restoreth my soul: he leadeth me in the paths of righteousness for his name's sake.

Renewing connects you to the God within, restoring your *Soul* back to its Spiritual setting. Renewing allows you to anew – you are leaving the chaotic mind set. Thus, becoming *Anew*. And, in your '*Anewness*' of your Spiritual mind, you are able to transform when you allow yourself to listen to the God Spirit within, which leads you on the correct path, the God's will path. This is how you transform this world to a higher state of Spiritual awareness, which allows you to see and meet your purpose.

What makes it possible for us to renew, is that God designed us with two parts. As stated in Chapter 1, the Spiritual part is encapsulated within the body part. And, a person cannot touch one's Spiritual part without one's consent. This means rape, molestation, verbal and physical abuse, mental and physical disabilities, disease (dis-ease), abandonment, etc. have no power or authority over you unless you allow it because we can enter into renewing our connection with God. Thus, allowing HIM to restore our soul. Yes, we can transform from the negative mindset of our human life existence to the Godly mindset of our Spiritual being existence.

Remember, there is a Spirit inside of you intact and ready to work on your behalf. A God's Spirit exists in you and it is ready to restore you enabling you to transform. All you must do is go through the process of renewing it.

Steps in renewing...

Step 1: Discernment – Stay away from negative people, places, and situations you can avoid. Discernment is a very powerful weapon in the fight against stress. Take time to learn the stressors in your life. Learn what things, people, and events distress you. Learn how you respond to them. Examine your reaction to stressors. You want your feedback to be calming and to have a positive effect on your body.

Step 2: Proper Diet – Get a thorough physical examination, and if necessary, have your doctor refer you to a nutritionist for a well-balanced, nutritional diet personalized for you. Individuals have different dietary concerns. Cholesterol, iron, and sugar levels are just a few factors contributing to your nutritional needs. Does your diet support your energy output? The answers to these questions will vary from person to person. You may need to fast and detoxify your body. In other words, in order to know what your body needs as an individual, consult with your doctor.

Step 3: Quiet Time – Become still daily for at least 30 minutes. Quiet time is when one becomes still. It may be as short as 30 seconds or as long as 30 minutes. Quiet time allows you to renew your spiritual understanding. You may pray during quiet time, talking to GOD. You may meditate during quiet time, listening to GOD. You may praise GOD during quiet time. You may feel the need to ask GOD for guidance and seek God for help. You may want to empty your body temple through confession and profession. Then, allow GOD to fill you up with spiritual guidance and understanding. Sometimes, you may just want to sit and be still.

Quiet time may be used for visualization. Picture how you want your day to unfold. Create in your mind a vision of positive events, which you want to focus on throughout the day. Keep this image in your mind, and center your thoughts on it.

Conceptualization is a power tool in creating your reality. Your thoughts have energy associated with them. Therefore, negative thoughts put negative energy out into the universe and positive thoughts deposit positive energy into the universe.

Keep in mind, **'Like Attracts Like'.** Remember, the Power of the Christ is within you. The Power of the Christ within you will go forth to bring into existence that which you think and speak. Overtime, you will manifest your thoughts into reality.

Quiet time may be used as prevention or an intervention. Before the ordeals of the day begin, sit and think about what may happen during the day. You may need to devise or revise an effective plan for the constant struggles in your life. You can prepare to respond positively to those challenges and not allow them to upset you. Visualize a positive outcome. Many problems that you contemplate have solutions; you just have to find them.

Step 4: Rest and Relaxation- Rest and Relax your body. Find time to rest and relax your body. Take up a hobby. Engage in activities that you find relaxing. At work, you may want to take leisure walks.

A parent disclosed to me her remedy for keeping her sanity and becoming emotionally sound. She embraces fifteen minutes of solace in her room before dealing with her second job at home. Others may find the need to decompress before entering the home, leaving the stresses of the day outside. Make your home, whether it's a house, apartment or dorm, a nurturing environment by creating an atmosphere that caters to the renewing of your spirit.

In addition, one may need to develop positive supportive friendships and relationships. Listen to positive uplifting music. Speak words of life. You will learn that the first step in rest and relaxation is to change with what and whom you associate.

Step 5: Exercise - Exercise to increase your energy level. Do you come in the house and nearly collapse? Do you quickly become tired and irritable? Are you barely keeping your eyes open while driving home from work, school, etc.?

If you answered yes, then you are showing signs of a low energy level. You need more energy. Exercise is a way to build your energy reserves. Consult with your doctor to initiate a proper exercise program.

Step 6: Sleep – Get enough sleep. Sleep is the most important curative process in the human body. In spite of this, the significance of sleep is benched by diet and exercise. Looking at advertisements, one will notice that those for diet and exercise far out number sleep ads.

Too many people are unaware of the healing events taking place during sleep. Shakespeare called sleep "nature's soft nurse," referring to its restorative effects on the body.

During sleep:
> growth hormones are circulated
> tissue and organ repairs occur
> the crucial immune system in regenerated

These are the steps in renewing, restoring and transforming you body, mind and spirit. Renewing, restoration and transformation will not take place overnight or within in few weeks. You want to dedicate yourself to the process of renewing to reach the levels of restoration and transformation. The Spiritual number for transformation is 40. In essence, it will take a minimum of forty days to transform.

Renewing is the process; *restoration* is the goal, and *transformation* is our outcome. When we change our mind-set through renewing, we are able to transform and change our thoughts.

The importance of Transformation
When we transform, we are acting under the awareness and law that the external world in not more powerful than the internal world. Because of our ability to transform, which means to change our thoughts, we can change our outcome.

Remember what we said earlier:

Proverbs 23:7
For as he thinketh in his heart, so is he...

In layman's term:
Thoughts become Words, Words become Actions, Actions create Habits, and Habits build Character, Character shapes YOUR LIFE.

However, transformation is bigger than the changing of the mind, i.e. *I change my mind; I'm not going to the store.* Transformation is bigger than that. Transformation is a changing of the mind-set, i.e. your belief system.

In layman's term:

When your 'belief-system' gets off track allowing you to believe that you are worthless, you'll never be anything, you have no purpose for living, etc., you must transform. You must not just change your mind, you must change what you believe about who you are. You are not nothing or just anything. YOU ARE A CHILD OF GOD.

You must understand that transformation is Spiritual. Anybody can change their mind and change their thoughts. But, when I change my mindset, my beliefs, I CHANGE MY DESTINY.

> *Your beliefs become your thoughts. Your thoughts become your words. Your words become your actions. Your actions become your habits. Your habits become your values. Your values become your destiny.*
>
> *-Mahatma Gandhi*

Exercise 10
We are going to work backwards.
Part A. Get a sheet of paper and create two columns. In the first column, write down what you are experiencing in your life at the present time. In column two, write down your belief, which led to the experience.
(Example: Column 1: Domestic Violence   Column 2: He or She loves me.)

Part B. MOST IMPORTANTLY: Write down if this belief is causing you to be abused, neglected, hurt, etc..

Part C. If the belief is resulting in anything that hinders life, we know it needs to be changed. Now, you will examine, analyze, and meditate about the belief. Write down everything you know about the belief pros and cons. Write down if this belief makes sense or if you are just using it as an excuse. Make up your mind to read books about the subject reflecting the belief.

Note: This is the start of changing your mindset, changing your beliefs. This is needed to change your destiny.

I find that there is a sincere lack of appreciation for thought, a greater lack of appreciation for beliefs and a far greater lack of appreciation for knowledge. The evidence in the world that people, especially youth, refuse knowledge and refuse to think about what they believe is dangerous and has demonstrated itself to be deadly among young people.

> Romans 12:2
> And be not conformed to this world: but be ye transformed by the renewing of your mind, that ye may prove what is that good, and acceptable, and perfect, will of God.

Notice the above scripture is not about the changing of your mind. It is about the renewing of your mind.

An understanding of the *'Power of Thought'* will change aspects of your *Life*.

For example:
*Deciding to move leads to a new house
*Wanting a different car leads to getting rid of the old car and buying a new one.
*Needing a change of scenery leads to relocating to a new city.

However, understanding the *'POWER OF BELIEF'* will change your *DESTINY*.

For example:
*Believing that you do not have to live as a victim leads you to seeking help and getting out of a domestic violence situation. You are changing your Destiny from death to life.
*Believing that God loves you leads you to seeking help and stops you from trying to commit suicide.

*Believing that you could have a better life than your parents who are on drugs leads you to getting a college degree or learning a trade.

Remember:
    'In Order to Change Our Destiny, We Must Change Our Belief'

You Are Blessed

You are blessed because you are '*of God*' and that is very powerful when you understand, fully comprehend, and unequivocally accept what being 'of God' really is. Because God's spirit is within you, you can connect to the ultimate power and knowledge source anytime and anywhere.

You are blessed, because you are '*of God*' and when you connect to the source of God within you, you can overcome anything through the processed of renewing, restoring, and transforming; there are no pre-set conditions on you, which you cannot overcome. You have the power to overcome and transcend above any negative condition.

> *Matthew 19:26*
> *But Jesus beheld them, and said unto them, with men this is impossible; but with God all things are possible.*

You are blessed because God has chosen you. You have been chosen for a purpose, which is unique, specific, doable and, as I have found out in life, requires help. It mandates you going to and connecting with God. Therefore, ask and ye shall receive.

> *John 15:16*
> *Ye have not chosen me, but I have chosen you, and ordained you, that ye should go and bring forth fruit, and that your fruit should remain: that whatsoever ye shall ask of the Father in my name, he may give it you.*

You are blessed because God loves you. God will love you regardless of what you do. He has unconditional love for you. His love for you does not waver with the wind. Therefore, do not substitute or mistake someone else's 'so-call' emotionally abusive 'going with the wind' love for the steady reliable unconditional Agape love that God has for you.

>Psalm 45:7
>>Thou lovest righteousness, and hatest wickedness: therefore God, thy God, hath anointed thee with the oil of gladness above thy fellows

The most fundamental significant reason you are blessed is vital to your existence; you are blessed because you are created in the image and likeness of GOD. Yes! You are created in the Image and Likeness of God. YES! YOU ARE CREATED IN THE IMAGE AND LIKENESS OF GOD.

>Genesis 1: 26-28
>>And God said, Let us make man in our image, after our likeness: and let them have dominion over the fish of the sea, and over the fowl of the air, and over the cattle, and over all the earth, and over every creeping thing that creepeth upon the earth.
>>So God created man in his own image, in the image of God created he him; male and female created he them.
>>And God blessed them, and God said unto them, Be fruitful, and multiply, and replenish the earth, and subdue it: and have dominion over the fish of the sea, and over the fowl of the air, and over every living thing that moveth upon the earth

God has not forgotten you. And, you must not forget HIM. To fear God is to have the utmost respect – a reverential respect. Have respect for the God that created you.

God has not forgotten you.
HE made you in HIS image.

God has not forgotten you.
HE embedded HIS spirit within you.

God has not forgotten you.
HE knows your comings and your goings, because HE is always with you.

God has not forgotten you.
Seek him and learn the voice of HIS spirit.

GOD HAS NOT FORGOTTEN YOU.
HE LOVES YOU - ALWAYS HAS AND ALWAYS WILL.
~Queen Phyllis L-Miata

Daily Affirmations for the Student
Author: Phyllis L-Miata

1. I will start in order to finish.
2. I will plan my work and work my plan.
3. I will create and seize opportunities to improve my life.
4. I accomplish all I want to do today with grace, love, and enthusiasm.
5. I believe that I can make it; I will keep on trying.
6. I choose thoughts and words that support and enable me to create the life I really want.
7. I will speak with and talk to others, the way I want them to speak with and talk to me.
8. I will set goals and visualize myself reaching my goals.
9. I will uplift myself when I speak.
10. The harder I work the easier the work becomes.
11. Daily, I will make and take paths to my goal.
12. I will act and treat myself the way I want others to act towards and treat me.
13. I will stay away from people and places where trouble exists.
14. I will protect my mind from negative and depressive talk.
15. I will be successful, for success is the best revenge. (Think about your high school reunion.)
16. I will not give up my power; I will not give up my control. (Good for when others want to make you angry or make you lose control.)
17. I will choose greatness.
18. There is only one of me. I am a unique individual; I am special in every way.
19. Whatever I desire is possible.
20. I have the power to make the changes that I need to make in my life.
21. I will not accept others low expectations of me as those of my own.
22. I set and live up to my high expectations of me.
23. I will control my destiny.
24. I will not leave my life up to chance.
25. I have the power to write my life and edit my story.
26. I will seek knowledge, wisdom, and discernment.
27. I will go for my dreams; I will make my dreams a reality.
28. I am fully in charge of my own happiness.

29. I am my own best friend-the person I enjoy being with the most. (Good for when you feel lonely.)
30. I am confident. I am victorious. I am a winner.
31. I am a beautiful/handsome person.
32. This challenge is only a temporary step in my reality; it is not my reality. I am thankful for the lessons I am learning.
33. I will protect my mind and my body.
34. I will not be a waste dump for other people's garbage, talk, and problems.
35. I will not judge people unless I have walked in their shoes.
36. Today, is the first day of the rest of my life.
37. I love you, but I love myself more. (Very useful when being pressured to have sex to prove love)
38. I am the only one who can accept and place boundaries on me.
39. I move beyond all limitations into a no-limit world. I achieve my goals with ease.
40. **I will not give up on myself. Every day, and in every way, I will make my life better and better.**

Products by PhyllisL-Miata
(Available for purchase online at www.PhyllisL-Miata.com.)

Next Recommended Book in this Series:
Permission To Be Great
Rise and Live in your Greatness

Book: **From Parent to Power**
Written for Parents, Guardians, and Caretakers

Book: **God Has <u>Not</u> Forgotten You**
Written for ages 14 – 24, but what everyone should know.

Workbook: **God Has <u>Not</u> Forgotten You**
Engages the reader of the Book: *God Has <u>Not</u> Forgotten You* to think, create, and write about their destiny. Puts the reader on the road to transforming their life.

Poster: **The Proclamation**
Daily Affirmations for the Student
<u>Description</u>
Forty inspiring affirmations for the student.

Card: **Daily Affirmations for the Mother**
<u>Description</u>
Size: 8.5"x5.5" - Everyday is Mother's Day with this card that has over 40 affirmations for the Mother.

Card: **Daily Affirmations for the Father**
<u>Description</u>
Size: 8.5"x5.5" - Everyday is Father's Day with this card that has over 40 affirmations for the Father.

Other Writings:
*In Challenging Times
*Through Challenging Times

www.ingramcontent.com/pod-product-compliance
Lightning Source LLC
Chambersburg PA
CBHW050555300426
44112CB00013B/1925